DEVON V

Devon
Villages

S. H. BURTON

ROBERT HALE · LONDON

© S H Burton 1973
First published in Great Britain 1973

ISBN 0 7091 3659 5

Robert Hale & Company
63 Old Brompton Road
London, S.W.7

PRINTED IN GREAT BRITAIN BY
CLARKE, DOBLE & BRENDON LTD.
PLYMOUTH

Contents

Illustrations

PICTURE CREDITS

S. H. Burton: 1, 2, 3, 4, 5, 6, 7, 8, 9, 10, 11, 12, 13, 15, 16, 34, 35, 36, 37, 38; Robert Howarth: 14, 17, 18, 19, 20, 21, 22, 23, 24, 25, 26, 27, 28, 29, 30, 31, 32, 33.

Acknowledgements

I have been greatly helped by Christina Corser, whose research on Dartmoor villages was invaluable, and by Robert Howarth who took many photographs especially for this book.

The Western Morning News, B.B.C., Plymouth and Westward Television have been vital sources of information. I have also relied on the work of W. G. Hoskins—his *Devon* is indispensable—H. P. R. Finberg, Joscelyne Finberg, A. H. Shorter, W. L. D. Ravenhill, K. J. Gregory, R. R. Sellman, Charles Whybrow, Ernest Martin, Victor Bonham-Carter, and A. J. Butcher.

I have based my chapters on the geographical areas described in the Devon County Council's *County Development Plan* (Second Review), a document widely and rightly admired for its clarity and good sense.

My thanks are also due to the librarian of St Luke's College, Exeter, to David Rees, to Norman Cole and to the headmaster of Spreyton Primary School for permission to inspect the school log books.

Introduction

THIS book has been written at a time when the villages of England—and particularly those of Devon—are being subjected to pressures that are changing these rural communities more swiftly and more fundamentally than at any previous period. Therefore, though I have not neglected historical description—for knowledge of the past is essential to an understanding of what is now happening—it seemed important to lay stress on current developments.

I have drawn attention to the geographical, economic and social background and thus tried to place the villages in their total setting. To do this it was necessary to write about them in the context of the county as a whole and then to narrow down the description to each of the sub-zones into which Devon divides.

Naturally, I have not been able to write fully about every Devon village. Faced with so large a territory, selection was essential, and I have attempted to highlight those places and features that are prominent in an often confused situation and to direct attention to aspects not always dealt with in guide-books.

It is my hope that the book will encourage its readers to make their own discoveries about the villages of Devon and that they will find it a helpful starting point from which to begin a fascinating journey.

S. H. Burton

I

Past and Present

HARVEST HOME in a Devon village. The celebrations begin
with a church service at two o'clock on the Saturday afternoon:
a Saturday in early October. By ten to two the little church is full.
It won't be more than a quarter full again—not even at Christmas
or Easter—until Harvest Home next year. Even the front pews are
occupied today. As a rule, nobody sits there because the fine
Jacobean screen is uncomfortably close to them. Today, the occupants of the front pews are faced by the marrows, potatoes and
apples lodged in the niches or dangling from the finials. Between
the sacrificial vegetables and fruit, wooden faces peer. Green men,
fish gods and dragons leer and grimace, huff and puff, at the human
beings so uneasily close to them. When these same embarrassed
people rise for the processional hymn, spiky oat straw and tickling
wheat ears brush against their faces.

The people in the front pews are 'foreigners'. Those on the left—
the lectern side—bought the Big House six months ago. Those on
the right—the pulpit side—bought the Old Forge at about the
same time and have spent several thousand pounds on it—bath-
rooms, fitted kitchen, woodworm and dry-rot eradication.

Both families are doing their best to integrate. They subscribe
to all the village activities; they have accepted various burdensome
offices and they are convinced of the necessity of helping to run
things and of supporting the rector. Had they lived longer in the
village they would have arrived earlier for the service and so
avoided their present very uncomfortable seats.

The rector is not preaching at this service. At Harvest Home the

village likes to invite a guest preacher. Rather special qualities are
looked for in Harvest Home sermons and the few parsons able to
meet these requirements are in great demand at this time of the
year. Thanks to the Almighty for his goodness are recognized as
being in good taste, but must be accompanied by lavish tributes
to the farmers' skill and hard work. It is generally realized that, left
to himself, God would make a poor showing. The preacher's skill
is especially taxed after a wet season, just as each year the
meteorological divinations of the Parochial Church Council are
severely tested when—usually about May or June—they decide
on the date of Harvest Home. "All is safely gathered in" sounds
doleful when rain lashes the church windows and lodged corn lies
in sodden fields.

Nor can an indifferent Harvest Home preacher rely upon his
congregation's undivided attention. The various fruits and flowers
rioting on screen, window ledges, altar, pulpit and lectern are all
being judged, weighed, even priced, by critical eyes. And, in any
case, the Saturday afternoon service is merely the prologue to a
varied programme. After church, the sports: held in a field belonging to the Rector's Warden. No Olympics these: but hotly
contested egg-and-spoon, three-legged and wheel-barrow races,
for which there are prizes bought by public subscription, as are
the barrels of beer and cider from which the adults help themselves throughout the sports. And in the evening a whist drive and
dance in the old schoolroom, in which most of the growns-ups
present received their education but which now functions solely
as a parish hall.

Next day, matins is well attended. It's the last act of the last
vestiges of communal drama surviving in a modern village. After
which the church reverts to its deserted state. For the next fifty-
one Sundays only a handful will be present, though Christmas and
Easter communions yet retain some hold on the allegiance of what
is nominally a preponderantly Anglican community. Nor do the
Nonconformists put up a much better show. A few years ago there
were several chapels, for Devon was historically a stronghold of
Dissent. Now, only the old Wesleyan chapel is in use and the combined numbers of the still-practising members of several sects
can fill it barely half full.

No squire, no school. The old people say that there's no leadership any longer. But even they don't take these laments very seriously. They are produced because they are expected. They know very well—and some of them will sometimes admit—that, materially, they are far better off than in 'the old days'.

The village still has its own incumbent, though you will hear it said that "you can't really call him ours any longer". Several neighbouring parishes are 'in the group' and three parsons do the work that six once did. One service each Sunday in each church is the rule. It may be communion or matins, or matins followed by communion, or evensong. "You never know which it will be," they grumble, oblivious of the fact that dates and times are posted on the church door and printed in the monthly magazine provided free to every house. "You never know," they go on saying. It's a heaven-sent excuse for staying away. You can't ignore the church in a village. It dominates the scene. If you are a native your family name appears several times in the graveyard. You are fond of the place, in a detached, unquestioning and undoctrinal sort of way. So it's convenient to have a generally accepted excuse for not going. "You never know. . . ."

The population of this village has declined steadily for the past hundred years. The loss of people makes it difficult to sustain village clubs and societies. Quite often, the cricket club has to cancel fixtures, especially at hay-harvest, because it cannot raise a team. Indeed, in several summers recently the club has been in abeyance, though even in those blank years it has held its A.G.M. in November, followed by dinner at 'The Bell'. The traditional meetings such as that and the annual parish meeting in March are still well attended. They are usually quite exciting, involving a good deal of politics. Village politics, of course; and therefore more involved and devious than the national variety, being complicated beyond a newcomer's understanding by an intricate network of blood ties—and feuds. Only that remarkable organization, the W.I., manages to maintain a flourishing life unimpaired by either dwindling numbers or internecine but enjoyable strife.

In general, however, the handful of youngsters look to the nearest market town and not to the village for their pleasures and their social life. They have to look outside the village for their work, educational reorganization has taken them outside the village for their schooling, so it was inevitable that they should look out side it for their relaxation. The newcomers are always trying to revive old activities in well-meant and doomed attempts to make the village more lively and to give the young people something to do. But a social club run in the cream and chocolate schoolroom and self-conscious imitations of the Whitsun Revels which died out a century ago are unable to compete with the coffee bar and disco a mere five miles away.

There is a much more serious problem in the village than the lack of former social activities. To find work and housing for its young people is the paramount need if the community is to achieve biological stability. The decline in native numbers has not made life easier by reducing pressure on living space or by increasing the value of labour through scarcity. Numbers have declined because the great primary industry, farming, needs far fewer men than it used to. And, when the old fulling mill by the river stopped working in the mid-eighteenth century, farming was the village's only source of employment. It was the farmers and their labourers who kept three smiths, two tailors, two bootmakers, six inns and one brewery in work. Some of the old men can tell you about those days when you sit with them in 'The Bell'. They can't remember them, but their fathers could.

The post-1945 influx of immigrants has done something to offset the population decline and has, of course, accentuated the housing problem. Property prices rise every year. By no means all the immigrants are retired. They travel daily to their work: lawyers, accountants, company directors. They buy houses at prices the local youngsters can't dream of raising and then spend as much again on improvements. It's no use 'blaming' them for this. The houses are on the open market and are worth what they can fetch. At least, there are few derelict dwellings to be seen now: no gaps in the thatch, no boarded-up windows, no nettles and brambles waving over crumbling garden walls. The village is launched on a strange new course, heading for an unknown destination. It's very bewildering after centuries of fixed and traditional life patterns, but it is by no means certain that change means death. Only of this can we be sure: the village is a radically different community from what it used to be. Its former economic and hierarchical structures survive vestigially: the appearances linger long after the vitality has waned. Yet the explorer of Devon's villages today may well find it as rewarding to attempt to discover the new growth points in these ancient settlements as to concentrate exclusively on the past and its imprints.

We cannot, however, hope to interpret the present without some knowledge of the past by which it was shaped. Nor can we know much about any village if we look at it in isolation. The villages of Devon root in its soil, bearing a general character derived from the county's topography, climate, vegetation, occupations and history. And, since the county itself is dramatically divided into distinctive zones, accurate observation and understanding of individual villages demand an awareness of the localised environment.

Although Devon is the third largest of the English counties in area it is thirteenth in population and has, therefore, compared with most of England, a very low density of occupation. Nearly half its inhabitants live in 10 per cent of the county. An unusually high proportion of its work force—nearly twice the national average—is employed in 'primary industries': a term that of course includes agriculture, in which industry, in Devon, three times the national proportion work. This scattered settlement pattern and the predominance of agriculture create the essentially rural nature of the county's life. In an age when Britain as a whole is becoming increasingly industrial and urbanized, Devon retains its country character.

Wages are low and seasonal unemployment is high, yet for many centuries Devon was a prosperous manufacturing and agricultural area. As late as the first national census of 1801 it was the fourth most populous county. Now, it is the most popular holiday land in Britain, attracting annually more than one quarter of those holiday makers who do not go abroad. An astonishing proportion which will undoubtedly increase.

Historians assert that almost all the place-names that we know today could have been inserted on a map of Devon by a cartographer working in 1350; and since *when?* and *why?* are the two questions that an explorer of villages must always ask, it is essential to have the outlines of the early settlement in mind. The traveller in Devon today sees farms, hamlets and villages of surprising antiquity. Whatever alterations time, fashion and

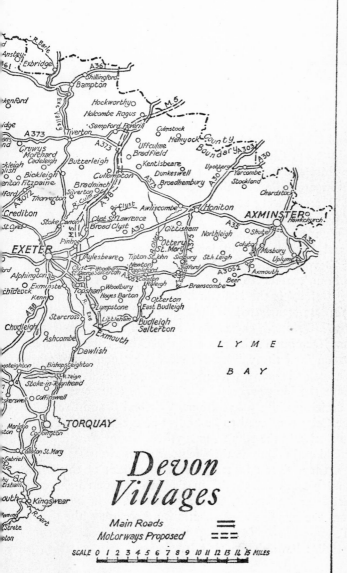

Devon
Villages

Main Roads
Motorways Proposed

SCALE 0 1 2 3 4 5 6 7 8 9 10 11 12 13 14 15 MILES

technology have wrought on the buildings, the occupation sites have not changed. There are, of course, some 'new' villages—mostly mining and fishing settlements—but the general pattern was laid down very long ago. To tell the story in full is beyond the purposes of this book, but the chief stages in the founding of the villages must be made clear.

The very name of the county provides evidence of the greatest importance: evidence that derives from the most formative of all the settlement periods; and evidence that directs our attention to the fact that Devon was for a very long time both a frontier and a racial melting pot. Nobody who fails to grasp that fact can hope to understand Devon village life.

The Anglo-Saxon Chronicle provides the earliest-known reference to the shire and its people by name. Under the year 823 the men of Devon are called by the chronicler 'Defnas', and in the entry for 851 an exciting story is told of a great victory which Ealdorman Ceorl and the men of 'Defenascir' won over a band of Danish plunderers. In the later entries the county is called 'Defnum' and 'Defenum'. (So long ago were the twin forms 'Devon' or 'Devonshire' established. Since the ninth century, in fact, it has been 'correct' to call the county by either name.) The tribal name 'Defnas' is the key word. As was common, the name of the people was transferred to the land in which they lived and so 'Defenascir/Defnum' came about. But 'Defnas' itself was derived from 'Dumnonii', the name of the Celtic tribe who were living in Devon (and throughout the south-west peninsula) when the Saxons came and made it part of England.

Throughout the long period of colonization, interspersed with sharp and decisive military operations, Celt and Saxon lived side by side. The Celts continued to be known as the 'Dumnonii'. The Saxons who settled in the county, using the spade or plough whenever they could and taking up their famous short swords whenever they had to, themselves adopted their own variant of the Celtic name, becoming known as the 'Defnas'. Both conquered and conquerers, natives and colonists, Celts and Saxons, went by a name deriving from the same word—a Celtic word meaning 'the people of the land'.

Recent studies have shown that 'settlement' is a much more

accurate term than 'conquest' to describe the coming of the English to Devon. The land was sparsely populated when they arrived.
Emigration of the Dumnonii to Brittany had been large-scale and
prolonged. Much land that had once been cultivated had returned
to waste. The great moorlands had been empty since the barrow-
builders left them. At lower altitudes there was much marsh, and
enormous forests filled many of the valleys. Land was there for the
taking with nobody to dispute the claim. Battles there were, of
course. Those fighting farmers, the English, had an eye to the fertile
Red Lands first. But they were soon at work in areas that the Celts
had never farmed, or busy reclaiming those once-productive acres
abandoned when the Celtic migrants set sail for Brittany.

Similarly, it has become increasingly clear that the theory—beloved of earlier historians—of a ruthless extermination of the
Celtic inhabitants of Devon by Saxon invaders is without any
reasonable foundation. The Defnas had no possible reason to
massacre the Dumnonii. There were, as far as we can tell, three
rapid and efficient military campaigns, and in between there was
a great deal of work to be done: work for which the Saxons needed
all the labour they could get. Farming in most of Devon has never
been an easy job. When there was forest to clear and swamp to
drain before the farming could begin it would have been extremely
foolish to reduce the available work force.

In any case all the available evidence points to considerable
Celtic survival. Although very few Celtic place-names still exist
in Devon it is clear that Dumnonian life persisted in the foothills of
southern and western Exmoor and in the uplands between the
rivers Exe and Teign. Another Celtic enclave was secure in the
Tavy valley and at least two notable settlements rode out the
storm in the shelter of Hembury Fort, the finest Iron Age 'castle'
in the county. The comparative absence of Celtic place-names is
no proof of genocide but argues much more forcibly that Devon
was very lightly populated when the Saxon settlement began. It
also, of course, concords with the known fact that the Anglo-
Saxon language rapidly replaced the tongue of the native Wealas.
Across the Tamar the Celtic language survived for some centuries,
but the Dumnonii of Devon soon adopted the speech of the
Defnas.

There is further and conclusive evidence. The existence of an independent Cornish kingdom and the mounting pressure of Danish invasion forced the kings of Wessex to consolidate their gains in Devon. A combination of firmness and tolerance, exemplified in the famous Laws of King Ine (688–725), marked their policy. Ine himself was the son of a Saxon father and a Celtic mother, so it may be thought that the work of reconciliation would come naturally to him. Enlightened self-interest played its part, however, in his reign and in others. The House of Wessex needed a loyal and contented Devon. The unquestioned allegiance of the Saxon settlers could have been offset by the smouldering resentment of the Devon Dumnonii. Yet neither the 'West Welsh' of Cornwall nor the Danish invaders ever succeeded in raising the Celtic Devonians against their Saxon neighbours. The successful 'Englishing' of Devon was the most formative and enduring influence on the county's character and life: a yeast that is still working. To understand its importance is to grasp the significance of attitudes and characteristics still present. The Dumnonii were notorious for their tribalism. Imaginative, poetic, religious, they tore themselves to pieces with their bitter feuds. Saxon steadiness, loyalty and practicality provided the ideal admixture.

The present-day pattern of Devon settlement cannot be better described than by using the words employed in *The County Development Plan* (Second Review) published by the Devon County Council in October 1970. The laconic language of the planners both sets the reader's imagination at work and provides the frame for the picture: "It is in the Saxon colonization . . . that the basis of the rural landscape of Devon can be found; large compact villages, many hamlets, and thousands of isolated farmsteads, and, by the time of Domesday, this colonization had transformed the county." And a map drawn from the known facts of this transformation enables us to read the minds and discern the motives of the Saxon settlers who, over thirteen hundred years ago, drew the outlines of our modern Devon village scene.

Based in eastern Dorset and using the sea as their highway, our English ancestors leap-frogged the Celtic defences. Wherever a river mouth afforded access they sailed inland and established their villages. Some have grown into towns, some have remained as the small, planned, rural communities that we still recognize as villages.

Up the Axe and the Otter first: Axmouth (developed by them from its Romano-British origins), Colyton, Otterton, Sidbury, Budleigh, Ottery. This sea-borne push outflanked the defensive works that the Dumnonii had built against the Durotriges of Dorset, and which Celtic feuds neutralized just when they were most needed to oppose the Saxon advance. Then the Exe lay open and shiploads of fighting farmers burst into and spread out from the tidal Red Lands, creating Kenton and Kenn, Exminster and Woodbury, and taking over the port of Topsham. Another leap took them to the Teign: Dawlish, Teignton and Kerswell resulted. The shelving beaches and rich land of Torbay were their next target as—two hundred years later—they were to prove irresistible to Danish plunderers. The great difference was that the Saxons came to stay; and here they established Paignton and Brixham, both of course destined to outgrow their villatic origins.

By this time, the success of the new colonies and pressure from the Mercians north of the Thames impelled the West Saxons to seek fresh expansion in Dumnonia. In the decade between 660 and 670 land-hungry bands burst through the Culm valley gap and swarmed down from the Blackdown heights. The northern prong of the advance took them into the fertile upper Red Lands. Hemyock, Uffculme, Cullompton, Sampford, Tiverton and Bradninch were secured. The southern prong took them to the old cantonal capital, Isca Dumnoniorum. Silverton and Thorverton resulted. They were in the fat country now and ready to push up the Creedy valley, establishing Crediton and Cheriton as firm bases and gazing with speculative eyes at 'the great wood' on their northern flank and the virgin territory to the south between Dartmoor and the sea.

Ten years later, they were on the move again. The fruits of settlement and woodland clearance had to be consolidated and the lingering remnants of Celtic military power crushed. In the far north of Devon they pressed along the ancient Exmoor ridgeway: a track over the high moors, linking the Cotswolds with far-away Cornwall. It had been a great trade route in Bronze Age days. The West Saxons called it by their own name—Harepath, 'military way'. They moved men and supplies along it so fast that the Celts were unable to offer any serious resistance. This push took them to

the north coast of what we now call Devon. Combe Martin, Georgeham, Braunton, Fremington, Pilton and Tawton were established.
They by-passed the Celtic settlements (Charles and Challacombe,
for example) in the Exmoor foothills, but spread down from the
moor itself and got to work in North Molton and Bratton (later
to be Normanized as Bratton Fleming). During the next three
hundred years these energetic pioneers moved inland from the coast
and north west from Exeter (Isca Dumnoniorum) settling the heavy
Culm lands—Buckland, Torrington, Beaford, and a score of other
places. They grabbed eagerly at the errant tongue of red sandstone fertility that pushes west from the upper Exe basin as far as
Hatherleigh and contrasts so dramatically with the old heavy soils
on either side. They took their axes to the great wood which
stretched from near Tiverton on the Exe and ran west to Morchard
Bishop. The Celts themselves had a few surviving settlements in
the 'Morchet' *(mor-cet)* such as Cruwys Morchard and Morchard
(Bishop) itself, but the new men hacked and cleared to such effect
that the map is now dotted all over with their *leigh, cot(t), cote*
and *worthy* place-names.

As the northern prong of the Saxon advance was pushing along
the Harepath over bleak Exmoor, a southern drive was completing
the settlement of Devon. Or, rather, successive and multiple
attacks were launched with the triple aim of securing the north-
west coast, of establishing a stable western frontier with the West
Welsh of Cornwall and of occupying the good land between Dartmoor and the English Channel.

The long journey through to Hartland was earliest begun and
first completed. Passing over the northern fringes of Dartmoor,
they wasted as little time in attempting to settle that inhospitable
territory as they had spent on the barren uplands of Exmoor. South
Tawton and Okehampton made useful bases, but Clawton, Holsworthy, Bradworthy and Hartland itself secured a line which, with
the trans-Exmoor drive complete, boxed in the whole of mid-
Devon. Thirty years later, they pushed down to the Ottery, a valley
that could be held; and Werrington, Lifton, and Milton developed
into those typically Saxon villages—part agricultural, part garrison
settlements—which formed the nucleus of the 'Englishing' process.
At the same time they were moving down from Exeter through
inland Torbay and into the district known from that day to this as

the South Hams. Here, and as far west as the lower Tamar, they combined land marches with ship-borne advances. The sea was always the Saxons' friend and the great estuaries of the south coast were their highroads. In general, they made their plantations inland from the river mouths, sailing upstream to the likeliest spots and making the wooded valleys ring with their colonizing axes. Chillington, Blackawton, Diptford, Dartington, Alvington, Modbury, Ermington, Yealmpton, Tamerton . . . the names tell the story plainly enough.

The cluster of Celtic place-names between the south-western fringes of Dartmoor and the lower Tamar is most revealing. Walreddon (south of Tavistock) indicates the survival of a Celtic—'Wealas'—settlement; and the name Wallabrook, (River Wallabrook, East Wallabrook, West Wallabrook) derives from *Weala broc* ('Welshman's brook'). Clearly, the Saxons, having secured the South Hams and curving round Dartmoor, felt sufficiently confident—and tolerant—to permit continuing Celtic occupation in a frontier area which might well have been expected to justify a policy of extermination or at least of forced migration.

A completed ring round Dartmoor, in the northern skirts of which South Tawton and Okehampton were already in being, and the basic job was done. Moreton, Brent, Walkhampton, Milton and—a vital strongpoint this—Lydford completed the new pattern. For many years to come, that vital western frontier was to shift: sometimes on the Ottery, sometimes as far west as the Lynher, and finally stabilized in late Saxon times on the Tamar. But except for this debatable land the whole of Devon was secure. The remaining three hundred years during which the house of Wessex reigned saw the peaceful work of colonization: steady clearing, tilling, draining, building. And, as importantly, saw the fusion of the two peoples, Celt and Saxon. When in 851, that band of plundering Danes marched inland from their beached longships just to the south of modern Torquay, burning and looting their way through the estates of the royal manor of Paignton—a richer countryside than they had ever known—Ealdorman Ceorl commanded soldiers who were neither Celt nor Saxon. It was "the men of Defenascir" who made great slaughter of the heathen men. In 838 Egbert of Wessex led the Devon men against a mingled Danish and West Welsh army at Hingston Down and "had the victory".

In 878, the bloody triumph of Ealdorman Odda at Countisbury, on the north Devon coast, signalled the end of King Alfred's darkest winter. The death on that day of 1,200 Danes put an end to any hopes their leaders had of raising the Dumnonii against the Defnas, of detaching Devon from Wessex.

It is the Devonshire Domesday Book of 1086 that throws the most light on what nearly four hundred years of Saxon settlement achieved. Despite the enigmas of that remarkable survey, its silences and ambiguities, it paints an informative picture. Two misconceptions are at once removed by modern readings of the Devonshire Domesday. Contrary to earlier beliefs, the Saxons *did* establish many large nucleated villages. The pre-Conquest pattern of Devon settlement was not solely that of scattered hamlets and isolated farms, though such lonely dwellings were and are characteristic of the county.

The term 'nucleated village' is derived by analogy from the life of bees. A nucleus is the centre of a bee colony. In a nucleated village, the people lived in the 'hive', had their farm buildings and kept their cattle there; and from there, as from the beehive, went out to work their fields. The nucleated village is *the* centre of the life and work of the parish which chronologically it almost always antedates by very many years. The non-nucleated village is simply the most important of several settlements in a parish. Another important distinction is based on relative siting, the nucleated village usually standing in the centre of its parish, the non-nucleated village often lying quite near the parish boundary.

It was in the lowland and more easily colonized areas that nucleated villages were planted. Where the land was poorest or the forest thickest, there people were forced to settle in small groups rather than in large clusters. It is because much of the Devon countryside is so intractable that the big village is not as common in this western county as in other parts of England. Wherever they could, the Saxons established the kind of village best suited to their kind of agriculture and to defence. The latter requirement explains why many of the nucleated villages originally belonged to the king and thus enabled their occupants to live the more securely under royal protection. Many that by the time of Domesday had been given to the church began as royal manors, passing into ecclesias-

(top) The green at Thorverton
(bottom) Berry Pomeroy church and rectory

A Devon village 'street', Berry Pomeroy

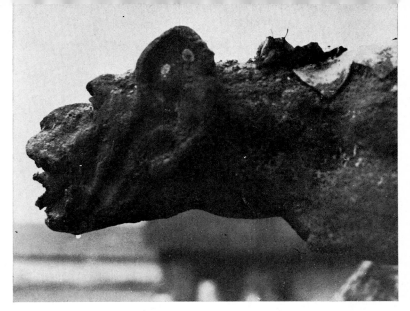

(above) The Winkleigh 'monster', a typical gargoyle
(below) Two inns at Winkleigh
(overleaf) Thorverton Mill

(left) Beech avenue, Chawleigh churchyard
(above) Steeply pitched thatch at Chittlehampton

Chawleigh: the school house

tical ownership only when the Devon settlement was far advanced and Celt and Saxon were one people. Similarly, the non-nucleated lonely settlements, unless they are Celtic, belong to the later stages of colonization when secure frontiers and a peaceful land permitted forest clearing and marsh draining and ground breaking by small groups of agricultural pioneers unafraid of molestation.

Also, we now know that the open-field system of farming was as well known in Devon as in the Midlands of England, where it survived much longer. It was the unusually early disappearance of the open-field system in Devon that led historians to suppose that it never existed. Again, of course, it was in the lowland and more easily farmed areas that open fields were established. In the tougher districts, small and enclosed fields were the pattern. Windbreak hedge-topped banks were needed, many of which survive to find their place on modern 6-inch maps.

The unusual mixture of open-field and enclosed-field farming in Devon demonstrated as early as the mid-thirteenth century the superiority of individual as opposed to communal holdings, while the insatiable demand for wool in later years encouraged enclosure and substitution of pasture for ploughland. By Tudor times the open-field system was a fading memory. It has been only in the last twenty years or so that aerial surveys and intensive study of Domesday have revealed how extensive the system once was.

Yet, if the farming system has changed and if the buildings themselves rarely go back much over three hundred years, the sites are the same and the village plans have changed hardly at all. The original houses were built of wood (the Saxon word for a building—*getimbrung*—means just that) and they did not last long; but the village lay-out was, in essence, indestructible. The detached houses stood alongside the village street or fronted the square or green. House and farm buildings, usually under the same roof, stood on a site called a toft. Behind the toft was the croft, the 'domestic' plot going with the site. Beyond the croft, usually long and narrow, stood the open fields (strip-farmed) and the communal meadow. From this farm land the crofts were separated by 'the back lane', a name perpetuated in a score of villages to this day. All round lay 'the waste', offensive to later agricultural reformers, but an essential element in 'old farming' economy, for it was on the waste that the geese and pigs fed and that furze was cut and turves were dug. It was very difficult to make any changes in a village built on this plan. Any alteration to a croft meant encroachment upon the street, green or square at the front or upon the back lane or the communal fields at the rear. The house might change but a complex and traditional web of law and custom defended the village ground-plan.

Domesday tells us something of what the Saxons had achieved. We know that the Red Lands of the Exe Basin were the richest and most heavily populated district, followed by the lower Taw and Torridge and the South Hams. We know that the Culm Country was the cattle raising area and was sparsely settled. We know that in 1086 Devon had very few water mills, and those all in the east along the Exe, Culm, Otter, Axe and Clyst. We know that there were still vast areas uncolonized and enormous stretches of woodland with little clearings here and there.

The next great leap forward came in the years 1150–1350 when the settlement pattern of rural Devon assumed its final form. (These were, of course, also the years in which the towns of Devon took shape, some to prosper: others—Rackenford and Noss Mayo are examples—to fail as 'speculative boroughs', reverting to village status.) This remarkable period was a sort of 'land rush'. In 1086 Devon was a poor county. By 1350 the foundations of prosperity had been laid: a prosperity that reached its height in Tudor days, declined rapidly throughout the nineteenth century, and has not yet been restored. It was all the work of free peasants. Obtaining a licence from the lord of the manor to 'prospect', they opened up the wilderness, broke the lower moors, colonized the heaths and swamps, established new farms, new hamlets, new villages, new towns. They created a new Devon and became themselves the yeomen of the county.

So far as our villages are concerned, 1350 marks the end of the formative centuries. A few exceptions—some of the mining and fishing villages, 'estate' villages, 'speculative ventures' such as Clovelly—do not weaken that general truth. The pattern that we see today existed when the Black Death arrived. It says much for the soundness of the planning—part instinctive, part theory based on centuries of practice—that the county recovered so quickly from that fearful visitation.

Both the topography and the climate of Devon are complex, while its geology provides some puzzling questions to which answers will not easily be found. Generalizations about the county as a whole are of little help to the explorer of its villages. A land in which the annual rainfall varies from 32·5 inches near Exeter to nearly 90 inches on Dartmoor; in which the January mean temperature at Tavistock is 5·4 degrees Centigrade and 3 degrees at Princetown, just over six miles away; in which February—the coldest month—can sometimes be as warm as April; such a land is not meaningfully described in generalizations. 'Mild and equable'? —true; of many places, often. Part of a great peninsula; nowhere in the county more than twenty-five miles from the sea; part of the Highland Zone of Britain; exposed to the Atlantic winds; having a north and a south coast; with an intricate drainage system; blessed with sheltered south-facing coves and valleys; much of its surface occupied by bleak moors and heavy soils—one cannot generalize meaningfully about this wayward land.

The explorer of Devon's villages must look at the soil on which he is standing and at the district to which he has travelled. Is this difficult country that had to be colonized yard by yard? Is this easy land that permitted the growth of large and clustered villages? Was this a village that was planned to provide security to men and beasts? Did this settlement spring up by a ford, a bridge or a cross-roads to nourish itself from travellers and trade? Is this village built round a central feature or does it straggle along a street? How can this site be best described: hilltop or spur, valley slope or valley bottom? To attempt answers to such questions as those is more instructive than to make sweeping statements about Devon.

Again, a knowledge of some of the basic elements in Devon place-names will often lead to exciting discoveries. Even the experts do not claim to know all the answers but the two volumes of *The Place-Names of Devon* will start the reader on a fascinating journey. A few examples will suffice. It is not perhaps surprising to learn that Alverdiscott was 'Alfred's outlying farm', but who was the Cnut who gave his name to Knowstone? Kelly is 'a grove', and Anstey means 'path up the hill'. Hemyock means 'ever-flowing stream', and all the *stows* are 'holy places'.

Detailed inspection of soil, site, plan and name comes vividly to life in the zonal setting, and since no book entitled *Devon Villages* can aspire to comprehensive accounts of even selected settlements, its usefulness and interest to its readers must derive from its attempt to provide a starting point for individual studies. Consequently, the chapters that follow are planned in accordance with the accepted division of the county into seven distinctive geographical areas; and each chapter is a beginning not an end.

2

East Devon

N o t so very many years ago, but long before the introduction of postal codes, it was customary for letters addressed to Tiverton and to places in its postal district to bear the legend 'East Devon'. How accurate this was, I never knew. In the sense that a great deal of Devon lay to the west of the Tiverton district it seemed fitting. But if we look more closely at the county's geography we see that Tiverton and its district are not, and never were, in East Devon: they are in the Exe Basin.

Inevitably, there are fringe strips—debatable lands—bordering each of the county's geographical areas; but an overall view of each zone reveals those distinctive features of geology, topography, settlement pattern, building materials, farming and—often —of climate that give it an individual personality.

For the purposes of this book it is legitimate to amalgamate certain sub-zones which geographers have, quite rightly, introduced into their specialized descriptions. A meaningful grouping of Devon villages, area by area, will then fall into the following zones: 1. East Devon, including Woodbury and its associated commons; 2. The Exe Basin, including Haldon; 3. Torbay and its sub-Dartmoor hill land; 4. The South Hams; 5. Dartmoor, including the Tamar Valley; 6. Mid-Devon, including the North-west Devon Coast; 7. North Devon and Exmoor.

The north, east and south boundaries of East Devon are unarguable, as a glance at the map will show: Somerset to the north, Dorset to the east, the English Channel to the south. But where, in the west, East Devon ends and the Exe Basin begins is occasionally difficult to define. Woodbury Common and its heathy extensions form a distinctive boundary in the south of the zone. Further north, the south-western spurs of the Blackdown Hills are unmistakably East Devon land; and though, hereabouts, the lower Culm valley forms an eastward-sweeping extension of the Exe Basin, above Uffculme the river's course lies in East Devon. The zone ends at the Burlescombe gap, the division between the Blackdowns and the Brendons.

East Devon, then, is a land of hills, its central feature being the irregular mass of the Blackdowns sprawling into Somerset in the north and down to the sea in the south, though cut through there by the Axe, Sid and Otter rivers. West of the Otter, Woodbury forms an outlier. East of the Axe, with a fine contempt for administrative decrees, the South Dorset Downs jut across the county boundary to form the third hill mass of East Devon.

More noticeably than in any other area of Devon, except the moorlands, the villages of East Devon are concentrated in the valleys, which tend to be steep-sided though flat-bottomed. There are exceptions, such as the tiny and comparatively 'new' village of Blackborough, high up in the Blackdowns; but that was a late creation springing up when whetstone mining brought an ephemeral prosperity to a lonely land. Blackmore's novel *Perlycross*, a much better book than *Lorna Doone*, though hardly known to-day, gives a vivid picture of life in those rough mining camps, few of which survived the importation of cheap foreign stones, and none of which remained productive after the invention of carborundum. Inevitably, many of the miners were Cornishmen and, a close-knit community, kept themselves to themselves, acquiring an unenviable reputation among their Devonian neighbours. It was freely rumoured that any stranger taking too great an interest in the pits, certainly anyone hardy enough to seek work there, was liable to be buried in the 'brekkles', as the waste tips were called, or flung down a shaft.

The whetstone mining was an expression of the varied geology of the area, the Blackdowns being greensand capped. Chalk creeps into the county where the west Dorset hills intrude and provides fine coastal cliffs of astonishing colours. The Axe valley is heavy with clay to the east of Axminster; but the mixture of marls and fine sandy soil in the lower Axe valley—as in the Yarty, Sid and Otter valleys—results in some good pasture and, in specialized areas, a high proportion of tillage.

The fall in cultivation and habitation as the valleys are left behind is most marked. The uplands with their grits, gravels, pebbles and clays are no more inviting now than they were when the Saxons laid the original pattern or when the free peasant pioneers filled out the landscape in the twelfth and thirteenth centuries. A good deal of coniferous afforestation, the disappearance of open fields, and the proliferation of Friesian milking herds would, of course, astonish a time-traveller from 1350. But he would still know his way around this countryside; would walk sure-footed from village to village between the Blackdown spurs; though he would be unlikely to take post-turnpike roads, preferring the familiar maze of upland tracks running through the furze and heather along Blackborough ridge or by Culmstock Beacon.

Another and pleasing result of East Devon's varied geology is the comparative frequency of flint as a building material. Cob and thatch predominate where local styles and antiquity still prevail, but the deserted sites of many small quarries remain to show where the chert, flint and sand were extracted and there are plenty of older buildings left to show to what good use the flint was put.

Any systematic exploration of Devon's villages must recognize not only the geographical areas already mentioned but also the smaller zones within those areas that topography, history, communications, occupations, or other factors may create. Just wandering is the most beguiling of occupations. First and vivid impressions accrue. You learn a lot and pick out places to which you must return. Those preliminary visits prepare the traveller for the delights that detailed knowledge will bring, when he has been able to concentrate upon smaller and cohesive districts.

In the north of East Devon lies a lonely, lovely area which can be isolated from the rest and systematically quartered by a zestful explorer. Let the Burlescombe gap be its western boundary; the Somerset frontier its northern; the A373 from Cullompton to Honiton its southern; and the A30 from Honiton to Ilminster (stopping, of course, at the county boundary) its eastern limit. Within that irregular rectangle lies a distinctive upland where, as compared with the rest of East Devon, settlement is scattered; and where those characteristic Devon habitations the isolated farm-house and the hamlet far outnumber the villages.

In making the distinction between a hamlet and a village it is not necessary to rely upon size alone (though a village is always bigger than a hamlet!); nor do we need to take into account the sophisticated refinements of definition which geographers must often employ. The distinction can rest securely on the basis pro-vided both by common sense and by that excellent book *Southwest England* (Nelson, 1969) whose authors state with refreshing simplicity that "some formal plan is the essential requirement of a village", and further describes it as "a nucleation of a large number of houses in a setting of streets, crofts and lanes".

Having discerned a sub-area of recognizable personality and of convenient size, the explorer needs a base: an exploration centre, which need not be central but should epitomise the district. The north Blackdown sub-area of East Devon offers at once such a centre: Culmstock, now so quiet a place, formerly a prosperous manufacturing 'town'.

Reference has been made to the comparative scarcity of water-mills in Devon Domesday. (The windmill, a later invention, never appeared in appreciable numbers: there was plenty of the right kind of water power in the county.) In the next two hundred years the deficiency was abundantly remedied. It is probable that in 1086, apart from East Devon, the county as a whole relied on the old-fashioned hand quern. But the development of the woollen in-dustry changed all that: hand querns would do for grist but not for cloth! The nearness of the main watershed to the north coast gave the south-flowing rivers a constant 'head', and the topography provided abundant breaks of slope. When, in the very early fif-teenth century, Western Europe discovered the virtues of a coarser woollen cloth, Devon—already the chief supplier of the home market—became the chief exporter, too. The frequency of the surnames Fuller and Tucker—fulling mills were often known as tucking mills in Devon—is a present-day reminder of the great age.

The earliest known location of a fulling mill—in which the cloth was cleaned and thickened by washing and beating—is Dunkes-well, not far from Culmstock. The date is 1238 and the mill was probably part of the abbey's property. Beyond conjecture Culmstock was listed as a cloth-selling town in the aulnager's accounts towards the end of the fourteenth century. (The aulnager was a sort of Board of Trade Inspector whose job it was to examine samples of all cloth offered for sale.) In 1394 these same accounts show that the fourth largest wool merchant in the whole of the county was a Culmstock man.

It is not easy to envisage today the effect of that woollen industry on what is now so quiet a countryside. Growing steadily throughout the later Middle Ages and attaining its zenith in Tudor times, the cloth trade of Devon was the mainstay of the county's prosperity and the support of its then comparatively large population. Perhaps we can best appreciate its importance by reminding ourselves of a description written by Thomas Westcote as late as 1630:

> First the gentleman farmer, or husbandman, sends his wool to the market, which is bought either by the comber or spinster, and they, the next week, bring that thither again in yarn, which the weaver buys; and the market following, brings that thither again in cloth; when it is sold either to the clothier (who sends it to London) or to the merchant who, after it hath passed the fuller's mill and sometimes the Dyer's vat, transports it.

What a complex organization and what busy comings and goings this exact description implies! Thriving markets, cottage industry, water-wheels turning, transport to be provided and routes to be maintained. In and out, process following process, and the pack-horse trains setting off for the capital, or the lumbering waggons creaking towards Topsham for direct export of cloth to Holland and subsequent distribution throughout Western Europe. Serges and perpetuanos; kersies; narrow-pin-whites; bays, single and double; lining-cloths; fine flax thread; bone lace; mixed coloured kersies; kersey stockings; shoemaker's thread . . . not an area of Devon—hardly, indeed, a parish—without its speciality.

Little new settlement was created by this roaring trade. Almost every one of the Tudor cloth centres was already in existence at Domesday. Water-power was needed, but Devon has plenty of that; and though the mills were not there in 1086, the power potential was. Here and there the centre of a settlement shifted from the hilltop to the riverside. Frequently, what had been a

C

village grew into a town; and just as frequently what had been a village rose, grew to the brink of 'township', faltered, lost momentum in the later seventeenth century—or held on until the Industrial Revolution—and then sank back to being a purely agricultural centre. Such a place was Culmstock. Such places, too, were Chulmleigh, Sampford Courtenay, Hartland, Harpford, Slapton, North Molton, Chudleigh, Moretonhampstead, Matford, Aylesbeare, Uplowman, and Bampton.

Others, of course, rose to the status and population of towns—and somehow held on: Honiton, Tiverton, Crediton, Barnstaple. They are not our concern in this book. Our business is with quiet, planned little places, many of which conceal beneath their bucolic exteriors the hustle and bustle of times past. And such a one is Culmstock, that ideal centre from which to explore the quiet uplands of the northern corner of East Devon.

Come to Culmstock from Uffculme; busy yourself with getting to Hemyock—and you will miss the main charm of the place. True, you will see the church; and that is a rare sight. You need to know nothing about architecture to realize that the Church of All Saints, Culmstock, is very unusual. There is a yew tree growing from the top of its tower and nobody knows how long it has been there. R. D. Blackmore, that incurable romantic, says of it: ". . . for a time much longer than any human memory, a sturdy yew-tree had been standing on the top-most stringing-course, in a sheltering niche of the southern face, with its head overtopping the battlements, and scraping the scroll of the south-east vane. Backed as it was by solid stone, no storm had succeeded in tugging its tough roots out of the meshes of mortar. . . ." He wrote that in 1895. Even Professor Pevsner struck a similar note in 1952: "All Saints [is] nicely placed just above the river Culm and its water meadows. The west tower would be quite ordinary . . . if there were not a yew tree growing out of its top at the meeting with the stair-turret. May it never be necessary to remove it!" And it is undoubtedly the one thing that even the hastiest passer-by of Culmstock must notice. But why not pull up and enter the church? Its finest treasure is its late fifteenth-century cope, exquisitely worked by the women of the parish to celebrate the building of the church, and now used as an altar-cloth. But those medieval angels and saints still sing and soar round the Madonna. A remarkable thing to find in a valley so given to the puritanical virtues. Remarkable, too, is the stonework that was discovered during the early nineteenth-century restoration: a stone screen, an armed figure and a lost tomb! It is more than likely that the Prescott tomb gave Blackmore the hint from which he developed the main plot of *Perlycross*. Certainly, his description of people and places have great life and authenticity. He was using material that he had known in boyhood, when his father was Culmstock's parson and the impressionable and sometimes lonely child explored the Beacon and the mazy lanes. He recalled in the novel his childhood terror when night fell and he had to pass through "a narrow and dark passage, arched with rough flints set in mortar, which ran like a tunnel beneath the first-floor rooms". Culmstock Rectory, he said, "was not a cheerful place to sit alone in after dark". A happier memory gave us "Crocker's Hole", one of the best fishing stories ever written. The giant trout lurked in a deep pool in a bend of the Culm, defying and challenging the anglers for miles around until two schoolboys overcame him. The boys in the story were, in real life, John Pike—one of his father's pupils at the rectory—and Richard Blackmore himself.

It was during Richard Blackmore's boyhood at Culmstock that the Temple family lived at Axon, a farm in Culmstock parish. Frederick Temple and R. D. Blackmore were at Blundell's School together, though Frederick Temple was the elder and in the sixth form when Richard was still a junior. Temple, his brother John, and young Blackmore shared the same lodgings in Barrington Street, Tiverton, and were thus able to enter Blundell's as day boys for the fee of £4 a year. Since neither the Temple nor the Blackmore family had any money to spare it was only in this way that the boys could get the kind of education relevant to their careers and socially acceptable. Though a rough school then, Blundell's taught well. In later life, first as Bishop of Exeter and later as Archbishop of Canterbury, Temple was generous in praise of his old school. Blackmore (who went "inside the gates", as he put it, after Temple left) was less consistent in his attitude. He immortalized the school in *Lorna Doone*, but though he sentimentalized many of his memories, his letters show that he remembered the barbarities and coarseness too.

The best of Culmstock, and the area most evocative of its past, lies north of the church. Down there by the river the plan of 'tofts and crofts and streets' is plain. I would always go this way to Whitehall and to Hemyock, rather than take the direct road. There really is a medieval feeling still where the houses cluster round the bridge; and it does not require much effort of the imagination to hear the bustle of the Tudor cloth market a little further on in space and time. It's quiet enough now.

Building is one of the few traditional occupations to have survived the economic storm that blew away the tradesmen and craftsmen of rural Devon. Many a little firm lingers on in the villages. Boots and bread come from the town, but the local builder is still a countryman. And he is truly *local*, rooted in the locality, knowing every house in the parish, for he and his father and grandfather have left their marks on every one. Such men understand the buildings in their care as big-town or even small-town firms cannot be expected to do. No job too small and none too big; though from time to time they have to leave you for a day while they build for a parishioner the last house he will ever occupy, for they are usually the village undertakers, too. Then the big shed at the back resounds late at night with the noise of saw, plane and hammer.

Thatch, of course, is different. Local builders will not tackle that as a rule, but the thatching grants have helped and so has the increased value of rural property. Consequently, there is a growing number of peripatetic thatching teams making more or less regular circuits. It is not nearly as difficult nowadays to get thatching done as it was just before and after the war.

The Kerslake brothers' building firm at Culmstock is a storehouse of craftsmanship and a repository of local knowledge: four brothers, each a specialist, yet each capable of turning his hand to anything. It is a joy to watch them at work and to listen to their stories of Blackdown land. Caring for the habitations of their own people has made them extraordinarily sensitive to the atmosphere and traditions of the upper Culm valley and its surrounding uplands. When listening to them I have often recalled without surprise that Thomas Hardy's father was a rural builder.

The 'back lane' way out of Culmstock runs close to what was once such a pretty and busy and self-important railway line. The Culm Valley Line—from Hemyock to Tiverton Junction. What

prodigality and confidence: and how civilized! Tiverton Junction;
a halt by the mill at Uffculme; Uffculme itself; Culmstock; Whitehall Halt; Hemyock. That was all. But think of what it did. It
linked the inhabitants of this remote Devon valley with the rest
of the great big world and provided them with easy, regular,
reliable, safe, cheap transport. And it didn't poison the environment, either. I would join any man in a fight to save elms and
hedgerows or moorland loneliness or rural footpaths. Why didn't
we fight for our branch lines and our slow trains? However did
we come to acquiesce in the insanities of closure? How did 'they'
ever manage to persuade us that the so-called economic arguments mattered? We were duped into being accomplices before
and during a murderous onslaught upon the quality of rural life.
If ever there was an issue on which the patient rural populace
should have spoken it was that.

Follow the dead line upstream. Come to pretty little Whitehall.
That new-fangled invention, the water-mill, arrived there comparatively early and revolutionized life for miles around. Wander round
and see the Domesday farms and hamlets: Culm Pyne Barton,
Gorwell Farm, Culm Davey with its ancient chapel. Look at the
quiet serenity of the Quaker meeting-house at Spicelands and the
much-disturbed exterior of the Prescott Baptist Chapel. Here, at
least, the renovators left the eighteenth-century furnishings.

Hemyock is known chiefly for its milk factory, and its economic
importance kept the Culm Valley Line open for the 'milk train'
long after its demise as a passenger-carrying railway. The whole of
the northern half of East Devon pours its milk into the Hemyock
factory—tanker-borne now. Its church got the full Victorian
treatment in 1847: they were so bad with their churches and so
good with their railways. The 'castle' to the west of the church has
been dated as late thirteenth or early fourteenth century and is
more accurately described as a fortified house than as a castle;
though it was strong enough to be used as a prison by the Parlia-
mentarians.

Further north, the long ridge of the Blackdowns shows that the
county boundary is very near. The streams that rise beyond flow
into the Tone, and what may, in this context, be called Devon's
last hamlet looks towards a Somerset sky. Clayhidon—some say
the name means 'hay hill'—is chiefly remarkable for its church.

Some trees soften the bleakness, but the tower gargoyles are frightening. The font and the pulpit are noteworthy, but it is the battered effigy in a dim recess that intrigues the visitor. It could be the representation of a priest called Ralph de Hidon. If so, it has been there for over six hundred years and—its features gone—it stares the gazer out of countenance, bearing so dreadful a weight of years.

Settlement south of the Culm is very scattered. What few villages there are seek shelter between the Blackdown spurs or along valley sides. Blackborough, as has been seen, is an exception; but even here some protection is afforded by the ridge that runs south from the Beacon. Saint Hill's exquisite little chapel is much more comfortably sited, well under the hilltop.

Dunkeswell climbs dangerously high up its hillside. On the bare plateau is a disused airfield and two miles north a disused and ruined abbey. The abbey—Cistercian—was founded by William Brewer in 1201. Brewer was a judge under Henry II, a regent in Richard I's absences, and a signatory of Magna Carta. He is thought to be buried here, but the story became very confused when Mrs Simcoe built Holy Trinity Church on part of the abbey site in 1842. Certainly, two ancient coffins were unearthed then and were thought to be Brewer's and his wife's. The church in the village itself is modern, too. St Nicholas's was completely rebuilt in 1865–8 but is noteworthy as being the home of a very ancient elephant. The Norman font, retained when the rebuilding took place, depicts—rather crudely, it must be admitted—a most unlikely group of figures, including a bishop, a doctor and this wholly unexpected Devonshire elephant. This is one of the earliest representations of the beast. It is quite beyond the most ingenious of interpreters to guess what that old carver was up to.

Rough Grey Bottom and a high bare ridge stand between Dunkeswell and Luppitt. *Lufa*—whoever he was—chose a fine *hollow* for his dwelling, and though Luppitt is a hamlet rather than a village it would be prodigal to allow the niceties of definition to exclude so delightful a place. This is wonderful country. The views from nearby Dumpdon Hill, for example, are very fine indeed. From the hill fort on the summit miles of the Otter valley unfold. The barrow-crowned Hartridge hills shelter Luppitt to the east; and Domesday farms dot the landscape. Mohuns Ottery, where the Carews lived until 1575, looks like a castle from a distance, and memorializes in its fine gatehouse the past splendours of the name. In Luppitt itself is a font that makes Dunkeswell's seem insignificant. A riot of carving—a centaur fighting two dragons, two men clubbing at each other with vicious bludgeons, long-eared animals, a totally uninhibited tree of life—has, like St Mary's magnificent roofs, brought fame to this tiny place. It seems strange to modern eyes that a font should be decorated in this way, but the work is very early (tenth century in all probability) and there were pagan deities as well as Christian to be invoked and propitiated. The marvel is that treasures such as this survived unscathed by either Puritan fury or Victorian propriety.

About three miles south of Luppitt, not far from the Cullompton-Honiton road, Combe Raleigh church provides a fine example of East Devon flint building and should certainly be visited; but there isn't a true village for another four miles. The route is up and down, crossing the long hill fingers: a countryside of bartons, hayes, turburies, barrows—and dominated by the splendour of Hembury Fort. When the village is at last reached the reward is great, for Broadhembury (named, like Payhembury, after 'the high burh') is one of the most famous of all the villages in Devon.

It stands at half the height of Blackdown top; and cannot be equalled for its pretty cob and thatch and general air of cosiness. Broad (Great) Hembury is very pleased indeed with itself and purrs like a kitten on a summer day. That excellent inn, the 'Drewe Arms', was very probably the church house originally, and it is heart-warming to think that ale is still sold where the Church Ales used to be held. The flavour and strength of the old brews were very different, of course. A present-day drinker might not be delighted with the ancient flavour—the 'Drewe Arms' was built at just about the time that hops were an innovation—but the strength would surprise him. It was a real 'nappy' ale; a quart of it was a dish for a king. Which makes it the more remarkable that in Chaucer's day and, indeed, right up to the Reformation, the Canons of Westminster each received a *weekly* allowance of forty gallons. Very pretty drinking! Of course, it was a 'perk' of the office and they were expected to sell some of it or give part away to friends and relations.

When church houses passed out of ecclesiastical ownership they did not always become inns. Some were sold off as private dwellings, others were used as parish halls. In their holy heyday the brewing and the consumption of the church ale were performed on the premises. The Church Ale (the *function* merits capital letters) was an annual event to raise money for the church. The churchwardens begged the malt from the farmers and then brewed it in the church house. Everybody in the parish came to the Ale. There was no incentive to stay away, since each parishioner was assessed according to his status and income and had to pay up whether he drank or not. Nor did how much he drank affect his tariff. In between Church Ales, the house was often leased to an ale-wife, a fact which naturally resulted in some of them, like the 'Drewe Arms', becoming inns.

The old distinction between an ale-house and an inn is worth recalling. It goes back a long way—long pre-1872, in which fateful year licensing hours were imposed on the sale of beer. An ale-house was not allowed to receive guests: an inn was compelled to. And to those far-away days belongs the honourable and ancient office of the ale-taster. He would enter the premises without warning, command a mug of ale and pour some of it on the wooden bench. Then he sat in the puddle, motionless, for about half an hour. If the ale had been adulterated with sugar his leather breeches would stick to the bench. We have great need of ale-tasters today to curb the evil practices of our monopolistic brewers. On the day I write these words it is reported that one much-advertised beer has fallen in strength by 12 per cent and at the same time risen in price by 40 per cent. That miserable potation would not have done at a Church Ale. The wardens would have been hanged.

Broadhembury's late fourteenth-century church has a fine west tower, typical of the strength for which Devon towers are famed and not without some of the grace which Somerset rightly claims; though not by any means the equal of Chittlehampton's masterpiece. The Drewe family (of nearby Grange) left their mark on the church. The south chancel aisle was once their chapel and there are two interesting Drewe memorials in the chancel. The Victorians left a deeper mark by their thorough 'restoration' of the interior. Here, they didn't do too bad a job; though it seems a pity that they thought it necessary to burn the rood-screen. There is a fine font with curious carving and the roof of the nave is unusual in having retained a lot of its original colouring. We are so used to white walls and brown wood that we forget how liberally the paint was splashed around in the Middle Ages. Toplady—the Reverend Augustus—was vicar here from 1768–78. He used to be famous as the author of "Rock of Ages", but he is forgotten by an age that doesn't sing hymns.

But it is as a whole that Broadhembury speaks to the visitor. Here is indeed a nucleated, truly Saxon, village. If anyone tells you that we don't have villages in Devon—the myth dies hard—direct his sceptical feet this way. He will return converted. My only criticism would be that the place is too tidy—too brushed and combed. Ungrateful of me, I know.

Grange, seat of the Drewes, a mile away, is late Elizabethan with eighteenth-century additions and 'improvements'. Edward Drewe bought the manor, which had belonged to Dunkeswell Abbey, in 1603. He already owned Sharpham and Killerton; but lawyers always do well, and Elizabethan lawyers did better than most. He could afford the place and the building which he at once put in hand. The plaster work is as handsome as the ceilings at Bradfield (near Willand). His son, Thomas, was knighted at Charles I's coronation and is buried at Broadhembury: "where be his quiddits now. . ."? Or, rather, where be his father's quiddits, quillets, cases, tenures and tricks?

The next village in north Blackdown land is Kentisbeare, and beyond that place the westbound traveller is heading for the Exe basin. Kentisbeare I remember with great affection as the gateway to the Blackdowns. It wasn't far from there, though many feet higher and after many a breakneck Devon bend, that I used to get my first glimpse of the thick cob walls and ancient thatch of Ponchydown Cottage. There, twenty years or so ago, I spent some of the happiest of my holidays and would then have been glad to settle in the remoteness of Blackborough top—but it was not to be.

Though so near to the wildscape, Kentisbeare lies snug in the Stoford water valley and waxes fat on new red sandstone. It's a world away from the pinched pastures and furzy hills that hang above it. One look at that handsome chequered tower, built of the sandstone on which it stands, is enough to tell the stranger

that there was no shortage of money when this church first started
to declare the glory of the Lord. One of its early benefactors was
John Whytyng. He built the south aisle, gave the screen, has an
altar-tomb in the aisle that he paid for, and used to appear there
in brass effigy until his image was discourteously removed in 1858.
He lived at Wood—one of Kentisbeare's nine Domesday manors—
and he was a Merchant Adventurer of London. The Whytyng
screen is the finest for miles around and typical in size and span
of Somerset rather than Devon. At the west end there is a most
beautiful gallery (1632) which escaped the restorers, no doubt by
divine intervention. On the floor there are hideous public-lavatory-
style tiles. Perhaps they were too busy laying these to notice either
the gallery or the screen. Yet they got half way up the walls in
places.

Near the churchyard is a building described by the experts
as 'the finest church house in Devon'. It is remarkable for being so little touched by chance, change, fashion or progress. Much
of the original medieval oak work remains.

From this delectable village some ancient farmhouses can be
visited: Orway, Saint Hill, Aller Court, Ponchydown. There is a
good public house and here may be enjoyed the pleasures inseparable from partaking in the life of a largely unchanging and still
independent rural community.

Though just north of the A30 and therefore technically within
the north Blackdown area already described, Upottery has a different feel. It is the first of the Otter valley villages that straggle
like sparsely-spaced beads on a long string between the Blackdown heights and the town of Ottery St Mary; at which point the
Otter turns south and interposes a flat-bottomed, steep-sided
valley between the Woodbury hills and the southern Blackdowns.
These upper reaches of the Otter and the triangle of lower land
enclosed by the A373 in the north, the A30 in the south and the
B3176 (Cullompton to Ottery St Mary) in the west demand separate treatment. Together, they form a distinct territory, based on
the Red Lands, steadily gaining height, steadily narrowing to the
lovely upland Otter.

Apart from its glorious site, Upottery's fame rests on the fact
that it was, intermittently it must be admitted, the home of a

Prime Minister. Late in the eighteenth century Dr John Addington of London bought the manor of Upottery and that of Rawridge on the other bank of the river. His son was Henry Addington (later the first Viscount Sidmouth) who was Prime Minister from 1801 to 1804. He built himself a big house and used it occasionally, no doubt finding life at Upottery a considerable change from London. The present manor house is newer and was built just thirty years before the church of St Mary (exterior, fifteenth century) was so thoroughly worked over that it no longer contains anything of interest. They did the same to Monkton just down the valley, though the Burne-Jones windows there, in the north and south walls, are held by many to be some compensation.

A mile or so north-west of Honiton, hovering on the brink of north Blackdown land and bisected by the main road, Awliscombe has a fine fifteenth-century church perched upon a hill slope and well above the village roofs. Like most East Devon churches it contains a great deal of Beer stone, notably in its north arcade and remarkable screen. For well over two hundred years, Beer stone—being easily worked and weathering so splendidly—was hauled all over Devon to beautify and extend parish churches as the money from wool became available. Naturally enough, Beer being itself on the East Devon coast, the greatest concentration is found east of the Exe Basin. Here, at Awliscombe, the masons brought the famous stone to life with their chisels. On the screen six angels support the rich tracery, the central arch blossoming with flowers that grew in the same architectural garden as the fleurons round the porch doorways. The Thomas Chard who made this beauty possible was born at Tracey in this same parish. He ended his days as prior of Kerswell (near Broadhembury), a cell of the Cluniac monastery of Montacute in Somerset, after being in charge of the parent house for some years. A pleasant semi-retirement which ended in 1541. Awliscombe stands on the river Wolf, a tributary of the Otter. About a mile above the village there is a triple fork in the watercourse, a feature that probably gave the village its name: 'the settlement in the forked valley'.

Buckerell, the nearest village to Awliscombe, defeats interpretation. "A very difficult name", states the standard authority—and leaves it at that. Due north, Buckerell Knap stands between the tiny village and the wilder Blackdowns. An entrancing road winds uphill between the Knap and Hembury Fort on its mighty ridge; and on, deeper and deeper into Blackdown land until, having reached the height of 896 feet just above Dunkeswell Turbury, it arrows across Blackborough top to arrive at the Beacon hard by the bare little church. Its height when it reaches Blackborough has deviated from that of its entry point by no more than forty feet in its three-mile run.

Buckerell is a pretty spot and its church has been much praised. Its best features are its plain eighteenth-century box pews and west gallery. Professor Pevsner refers to Admiral Grave's memorial as "a mourning female in relief seated in a roundel, and eagle above. . . ." Whatever it *looks* like, it was *meant* to represent Britannia with a dove! It was the work of John Bacon (1792), an artist much in fashion, who, having won a great many public competitions, was commissioned to sculpture memorials that found their way into Westminster Abbey and St Paul's. Admiral Graves retired to Hembury Fort House after conducting so unsuccessful a blockade of the port of Boston (a measure following the famous Tea Party) that he was suspended. Perhaps we may regard the 'mourning female' as a weeping Britannia.

For so tidy a place is Feniton—which would be barely a mile from Buckerell if English lanes ran as straight as Roman roads—the incongruity of a battlefield in the parish seems absurd. The village itself is neat and cared-for; the immediate countryside seems far away from Blackdown wildness; Feniton Court has a bland air of late Georgian complacency. Yet, down by the Otter in a field north of Fenny Bridges, the pitifully ill-equipped 'army' of the western rebels was defeated in 1549 by an efficient band of Italian and German mercenaries sent down from London under Lord Russell. The rebels were 'up' in protest against the introduction of the first Prayer Book in English; but the so-called 'Prayer Book Rising' was the culmination of years of bitter discontent aroused in the common people as they saw monastic lands sold off to local bigwigs and 'up-country' speculators. Lord Russell—formerly John Russell, a Dorset squire—had received the biggest plum of the lot, the estates of Tavistock Abbey, so it is not surprising that he fought this battle and later ones with zeal—and celebrated his victories with extreme brutality towards the conquered.

Devon's best historian considers it likely that this low-lying ground by Fenny Bridges also played a crucial rôle in one Saxon push against the Dumnonii. Professor Hoskins argues most convincingly that a Celtic flank was turned here and the Otter defensive line, backed by the chain of hill forts, neutralized.

Back in Feniton itself, there is a macabre monument in the lovely church. Thirteen Malherbes owned the manor in succession and it is thought that the grim 'gisant' in the chancel represents the corpse of the last in the line. (There are two of these cadavers in Exeter Cathedral, by the way, and they may be commoner than my experience suggests. Skulls, of course, abound in monumental mockery.) This particular 'gisant' has its shroud pulled aside and it really is very difficult to repress a shudder at the sight of this ghastly reminder of the fate we all must share. Precisely, of course, the intention. Perhaps churches shouldn't be too beautiful! Or perhaps they should mingle terror with beauty.

There is some very good modern carving in Feniton church and of a most unusual kind. Some of the sixteenth-century bench-ends survived the religious storms, and modern ones were designed to fill the gaps and match those that remained. They are excellent; and the achievement is the more remarkable in that traditional subjects (for example, St Michael weighing a soul) were chosen. This is the sort of thing that hardly ever comes off. All in all, Feniton would make a good starting place for the exploration of the villages of mid-East Devon.

Somebody called Paega must once have owned the manor at Payhembury, for both he and the great earthworks at Hembury Fort are memorialized in the name. Standing on a branch of the river Tale, an easy-going stream that joins the Otter half a mile from Ottery St Mary, it is tightly grouped round a street plan that looks like an irregular capital *H*. It has held on to life with astonishing tenacity, its population—apart from the peak year of 1851—remaining steady at around four hundred. Down the Tale valley there are some revealing place-names: Tuckmill Farm, Talewater Mill and—not far from the junction with the Otter— Woodcote Weir. This was a busy place at the height of the woollen trade and it was this wealth that built the Beer stone arcade and installed the superb screen in the church. The story is made perfectly clear in the contrast between the plain, rather austere, little west tower and the decoration of the beautified west doorway and of the added south porch. These later works were undertaken when there was a lot more money about. There is the usual Devon stair turret, but distinguished by a bell the inscription of which proclaims that "there is no better bell beneath the sky". Whatever the merit of that claim, the medieval glass in the north aisle is said to be among the best in Devon. It is often forgotten how little of the old stained glass survived the religious troubles. Payhembury can certainly count itself fortunate to have such a fine collection of colourful saints: St Vincent, St Blaise, St Stephen and St Laurence are all resplendent here.

Round about are some ancient farms, all within the parish. Higher and Lower Tale are all mentioned in Domesday, and Uggaton was a comparatively near-miss, being first included in written records in 1196.

Some of the local names, too, repay study, for they present even the experts with many problems. The river itself is rather a mystery. It should mean 'quick, active, swift' but its present-day gait would not suggest that this explanation is accurate. Not far from its junction with the Otter stands the superbly-named Clapperentale Farm. This was once known as 'Clobbere Thale'. 'Thale' undoubtedly comes from the river's name, and 'Clobbere' probably derives from its occupiers in 1302. If that is so, then the people who lived there so long ago were nicknamed 'clobberers' or 'clubbers' because they were, as the saying went, 'tall men of their hands' and quick to use their cudgels. The modern version of the name disguises this intriguing detail and has obviously been influenced by the clapper bridge.

Across the river from Clapperentale stands Escot, hardly meriting village status but remarkable for its antiquity (it was first mentioned in 1227); its achievement of parochial status (in 1840) despite its lack of size; and its legendary connection with John Locke. Sir Walter Yonge built a house at Escot in 1688 and Locke is said to have been a frequent visitor, memorializing his holidays there by planting clumps of beeches in the park. How one would wish to know which of those still-living trees were planted by that long-dead great man! How pleasant to imagine that this quiet East Devon countryside retains a memory of "that most modern and reasonable of philosophers, Mr Locke".

Talaton, though the truth of the explanation takes time to sink in, gave Escot its name. *Cot(t)* and *cote* names are comparatively rare in East Devon. They predominate in the poorer northern and western regions of the county where sparse settlements, dictated by thin soils and forest cover, made the outlying farm (which is what *cot(t)/cote* means) so characteristic a feature. Nevertheless, Escot means 'the outlying farm east of (Talaton)'. *Ton* is an enclosure or farmstead and Talaton itself is, therefore, 'the farm on the Tale river'. It is, in fact, debatable whether it does not more properly belong to the Exe Basin. It stands on a smiling hillside and shares many of the Exe Basin characteristics, but I think that its river name may permit its grouping with the East Devon villages. Feet lower and yards east, the Exe Basin demonstrably begins: thus fine is the distinction. It is a neat landscape here. Blackdown ruggedness seems leagues away. Cob and thatch, warm red sandstone barns, an easiness in the atmosphere: all this coming together most dramatically in St James's church, where, despite extensive mid-Victorian messing about, the confidence, energy, prosperity and good taste of fifteenth-century Devon still speak to us. That beautiful tower reads to even the most casual of visitors its sermon in stone.

Historically, there are four access points into East Devon (they have been of historical significance and remain vitally important because of the topographical features that they follow), and the east-west lateral run of each frames a distinct sub-zone of the area. In the north, as has been seen, the Burlescombe gap (A38 road and Taunton-Exeter railway line) marks the frontier of East Devon as a whole, curving south and running through the Exe Basin. The A30 and A303 roads cross the eastern Blackdowns and converge on Honiton. The A358 and the A373 meet at Axminster, traversing the Axe gap and, in their turn, lead to Honiton. The A35 enters the county west of Lyme Regis and demarcates a thin coastal strip on its up-and-down and lovely route to Exeter.

The junction of the A30 and the A373 at Honiton, with an eastern base on the county boundary, bites out a hilly and distinctive sub-zone of East Devon. Yarcombe and Stockland may be seen as epitomising the villages of this switchback country. Yarcombe means 'the settlement in the valley of the river Yarty'. According to one authority, Stockland means 'the land covered with stocks or stumps'—in other words, cleared land. Others think that it means 'the land of scattered stock farms'. It comes to much the same thing. Stockland parish is dotted all over with lonely farms and tiny hamlets linked by winding lanes; typical in other words of land won yard by yard from the forest. Stockland itself is very much the centre of this area, though Dalwood was a post-Domesday clearing colonized from Stockland, the parent settlement. Until 1842, incidentally, both Stockland and Dalwood were administratively part of Dorset and yet totally enclosed by Devon. In Stockland the bridge at the village end used to mark the county boundary. It is one of the numerous West Country bridges carrying a notice threatening dire penalties—including transportation for life—for damage wilfully caused to the structure. No visitor could fail to be pleased with this lovely little place, the traditional twin centres of which—inn and church—are worth more than passing attention. But perhaps the most striking feature of all lies high above the village. Here on a steep, bare slope, just below the long ridge of Stockland Hill, the Dumnonii built Stockland Great Castle as a link in the defensive chain that they constructed against their hostile kinsmen, the Durotriges of Dorset. The single wall of this huge fortress is still a very impressive sight, though the feet of time have been trampling it down for nearly 2,500 years. Defences such as these, tactically sited as they were, crowned with a (long-perished) wooden palisade, and reinforced by tall towers from which slingsmen poured a hail of missiles, must have seemed impregnable.

And on this same ridge today stands a television and radio transmitter from which all I.T.V. and B.B.C. programmes in colour, black and white, and sound go out to the whole of eastern Dumnonian and western Durotrigian territory.

Yarcombe, with which Stockland has already been compared, owes its present character to the 'new' road on which it stands: the Honiton-Chard (A30) road, cut in the early nineteenth century. The Yarty valley is overhung on both sides at this point—a five-hundred-foot climb to the west (where a curving continuation of Stockland Hill dominates the skyline), a four-hundred-foot climb eastwards to daunt the Somerset-bound traveller. An enormous bend in the road is a dramatic reminder of the problems that the surveyors encountered, and the village itself stands on this

Village street at Sandford

(above) Thatching at Puddington

(right) Stoke Gabriel church from the quay

Ashton, across the river

Cottages at Ringmore

great hairpin. Drake bought the manor and his descendants owned it for 350 years. The church—a flint stucture—belongs chiefly to the fifteenth century, but was badly served by a late nineteenth-century restoration. The Yarcombe inn was once the church house. These are historical facts, yet how little they tell us. That new road was far and away the most important in Yarcombe's story.

Below Stockland the Yarty valley opens out briefly. Where it is again pinched into a defile, Membury stands on guard. It is difficult to avoid military metaphors when describing Membury. Its name—a hybrid Celtic-English formation—means 'the stone fort' and refers to the enormous Iron Age earthworks commanding the high ground between the Axe and the Yarty rivers. This is yet another astonishing and enduring memorial to Celtic feuds, its blind-alley trap being a particularly cunning device. East of Membury the Romans ran a southern spur of the Fosse Way to connect with the port of Axmouth. In Membury parish itself a Roman villa was discovered in 1914. In the pretty church, which contains an unusually large amount of pre-fifteenth-century work, there is a memorial to Sir Shilstone Calmady, who was killed in a skirmish nearby in 1646. He was fighting for the Parliament but was nevertheless buried in the chancel. There are Fry memorials, too, for Nicholas Fry, who was Sheriff of Devon in 1626, built Yarty House and his descendants were there for a very long time. Seventeen-year-old Frances Fry, who died in 1723, got a particularly pretty period piece:

> Stop Passenger and view ye mournful Shrine
> Which holds ye Reliques of a Form Divine
> Oh she was all perfection, Heav'nly Fair
> And Chast and Innocent, as Vestals are. . . .

Chardstock is the only other considerable village in this sector of East Devon. It hasn't been in Devon all that long, having been transferred from Dorset in 1896, when quite a bit of boundary tidying took place. In a way this wasn't the tidiest of moves, historically, since Chardstock was 'the cattle farm belonging to Chard' and ought therefore to have rejoined its parent settlement in Somerset. But the names, of course, are much older than the counties. The countryside is very pleasant here: the deep Devon valleys and steep hills are beginning to open out and mingle

D

delightfully with knobby Dorset and the rolling Somerset uplands.
There's a lot to see. Chardstock Court used to be a manor house
belonging to the bishops of Salisbury. Much of it was built in the
early fourteenth century. Coaxden Hall was the birthplace of the
famous antiquary Sir Simonds D'Ewes (1602–50). Tytherleigh,
Cotley, Hook and Woonton have all been there since   at least
Henry II's time. And when these have been loóked at and the
church—rather savagely dealt with in 1863—has been seen, the
best exploring of all lies ahead, for Chardstock has two very
picturesque inns.

The sensitive traveller who is in tune with village life will not
need telling that the pub can be a treasure house. Two different
approaches are needed: go in during the morning and talk to the
landlord; go in at night and listen to the company. The latter
almost always works; the former usually, though occasionally the
man behind the bar is a newcomer and neither knows nor cares.

The A358 joins the A373 at Axminster and then, merged in the
latter road, follows its hilly course to Honiton. To the south of
this route lies a distinctive area of East Devon, split vertically by
the lower courses of the Axe, Sid and Otter rivers, all of which are
thickly dotted with typical broad-bottom valley settlements. In
between are high plateaux where hilltop villages are sparsely
spread. At its eastern extremity lies a curious land—containing
only one true village, Hawkchurch—which joined Devon only in
1896. At the western end, Woodbury and its fine commons make a
clear division between East Devon and the Exe Basin.

Hawkchurch is an intriguing name. The first element is the
Anglo-Saxon *heafoc* and it was in all probability a personal rather
than a zoological name. If this surmise is correct, then there was
a church and a settlement here in pre-Norman times. Who Hafoc,
nicknamed 'the Hawk', was we cannot know; but there is so much
of the *Norman* interior left in this hillside church, nestling just
under the high points, that it can be supposed that Hafoc's eyrie
was of sufficient secular and ecclesiastical importance for the new
men to continue and to develop settlement on the site that he had
chosen. Nor was Hafoc the first to appreciate this beautiful land
with its fine views over the Axe valley. Less than two miles south-
east, and only just within the Devon border, Lambert's Castle

crowns a hilltop; though whether this was built by the Dumnonii against the Durotrigians or the other way round is now past the wit of man to tell. It probably changed hands a good many times.

Back in the village, the remarkable west tower looks Somerset in style rather than either Devon or Dorset. The arms of Cerne Abbey on the tower and the quaint and highly secular carvings on some of the Norman capitals and archways hint at mysteries not yet solved. What exactly the whispering (or menacing?) serpents signified we shall never know, though the orthodox symbolism of the Fall may well have been the carver's aim. Nearby Wyld Court is far from enigmatic: good solid Elizabethan affluence here.

When the traveller can tear himself away from this hilly Devon-Dorset borderland he must drop down into the Axe valley and follow the river to the sea. Below Axminster itself, the river winds through a valley as near approaching a flood plain as Devon rivers ever achieve. Once, right up to Musbury, there was anchorage for ships. Even after those days, Axmouth was an important harbour.

Musbury takes its name from the Iron Age fort on the hill above the village, so the *bury* part of both names is clear enough. *Mus* is baffling. It means 'mouse', and the authors of *The Place-Names of Devon* suggest that it was "used in the compound to describe a deserted spot". Well, they are the experts. I certainly can't improve on their guess. The village is delightful, climbing gradually to its church and sheltered by its 'castle'. Below is the wide and pastoral plain of the Axe. Historians, amateur and professesional, can delight in the Drake associations and monument—these Drakes were a branch of Sir Francis's family and lived in nearby Ashe House. It is commonly believed that John Churchill, first Duke of Marlborough, was also born there after it had passed into Churchill possession, but since the Royalists burned it down in 1644 this is not very likely. He was probably born at Great Trill in Axminster parish. The present Ashe House was rebuilt in the years 1670–80. Enough has perhaps been said to indicate that any explorer of East Devon would do well to settle at Musbury for a few days.

Or Axmouth? Incomparable Axmouth. What a royal history it has had. The southern terminus of the Fosse; then a key Saxon settlement, passing eventually to King Athelstan; from him to Edward the Confessor, and from the Saxon monarchy to the Nor-

man. It was a prize in those days, though a modern visitor might
not easily see why. The solution of the problem may be found in
Leland's description (1538): "the river Axe is dryven to the est
point of the haven and ther, at a very smaul gut, goith into the
sea". Landslips—common all along this coast—and the pebble
ridge were the cause of the decline. Soon after the Conquest part
of Haven Cliff slid into the sea and the tides piled up the shingle.
By the early thirteenth century the once-splendid port was "a
mene thing", and though indulgences were offered to those who
would help to clear it these pious efforts were of no more avail
than eighteenth- and nineteenth-century ventures. Squire Hallett
of Stedcombe Manor was the last of a long line of pioneers who
tried to restore vanished glories. In his day, from a deepened harbour and a new pier, two schooners sailed regularly to London.
Coal and lime came in; hides and pebbles were exported. In 1867,
however, a single-track railway reached Seaton; and ten years later
Axmouth harbour was dead commercially. This was the port from
which the Romans shipped Cotswold wool and Mendip iron. They
settled this area, too. It suited them. They established villa life
here on a scale unknown anywhere in Devon.

Ironically, the pebble ridge that killed the port is a source of
income today. The stones are scooped up, graded, and used in
paint 'blinding' processes and rubber manufacturing

The life of the place has retreated up the valley, away from
the once-busy harbour (excavations have proved the former existence of a large population). Now, there's a cluster of cottages, the
admirable Harbour Inn, and St Michael's lovely church—more
varied in its styles than most Devon churches. Substantial Norman
remains—especially that great doorway—ancient paintings, a
priest who has been dreaming for as long as the port has been
declining. Words cannot do justice to Axmouth or to the Devon
chalk around, of which it is the unchallenged centre.

Uplyme, to the east, seems only accidentally in Devon so near
is it to Dorset and so grey its cottages. Not that it lacks charm,
but that this strip of borderland seems free of county affiliations.
There would have been a case for taking the Axe as the county
boundary for, centuries ago, it separated the Dumnonii from the
Durotriges and, centuries later, it was the line on which the dis-
united Celts vainly hoped to stand against the Saxons.

Colyford, north west of Axmouth, is as clearly Devonian as Up-lyme is a border village; yet it, too, is a gateway—to Colyton. Too large to be fitly included in a book about Devon villages, Colyton is yet so rich in history, architecture and character that the explorer of East Devon may well come to rest here for a time and make his forays from this place which, with sawmills, corn-mills, tannery and iron foundry, achieves that rare feat in modern Devon of being utterly welcoming to the visitor without feeling any sense of dependence.

Farther up-river, and westwards in the hills, lies Shute where the Bonvilles disputed supremacy with the Courtenays for a large part of the fifteenth century. It is all very baronial, for Sir John Pole brought it in 1787 and built Shute House over the next three years, new work mingling with the old. It finally became a rather nice girls' school of the kind that Devon specializes in. The county harbours a great many lost causes. The church is mostly Pole and quite dominated by the statue of Sir William in his costume as Master of the Household to Queen Anne. Shute as a whole is a period piece—of many periods. Deer Park to the west and Shute House park land to the east, the tiny village is uncomfortably squeezed between the two.

Southleigh and Widworthy, a little west, are more attractive because less shackled. Both are set in excellent East Devon countryside. Southleigh is very scattered. The Saxons worked hard for this land. But the little flint church perched on the combe edge and the pleasant countryside south of the Coly river give few obvious signs today of past struggles, either military of agrarian. Yet Blackberry Castle nearby ('the black fortress') and the place-names 'Harepath' and 'Ridgway' tell a vivid story to those who can read it. The leap across the Axe was a major strategic victory for the English: and then came the years of settlement while forest clearings were made and farms established in land that the Celts had never used. In this area the bases had to be secured, for there was now only one barrier left between the Saxons and the rich Red Lands that lay to the west. After the Axe, the Otter; after the Otter, the Exe Basin.

Northleigh is Southleigh's twin. ('Leigh' is *leah*: 'clearing'). Again, there's a church very largely built of local flint. The wood-work—bench-ends and screen—are particularly fine. But it is the site and the lay-out that so vividly echo Southleigh. Remote and quiet as these little places are, they interpret the remote past most strikingly.

Widworthy overlooks the Umborne Brook and lies close to the A373. It has the inevitable 'camp'—inevitable and ineffective, as things went—and a 'great house': Widworthy Court. Yet somehow, it's those disused quarries north-west of Sutton Barton that speak most vividly of the past. For here was once obtained a freestone rivalling in quality, though not in quantity, the famous stone of Beer.

Chalk appears for the last time in Devon where the great bulk of Beer Head rears over the sea, giving shelter to a fishing village of immense charm. Beer, like nearby Seaton (which has outgrown village status), was discovered by visitors when the railway reached the more popular resort in 1868. So, for a good many years now, fishing and 'freighting' have been twin occupations. (The term *freighting* is applied locally to the summer trade of taking visitors for sea trips.) It is not easy for strangers to imagine the hardships of the inshore fisherman's life. Today, the summer and temporary resident sees only the idyllic aspects, while the fashion for idealizing the 'pre-acquisitive age'—the back-to-the-spinning-wheel unreality of some leading educationists and sociologists—either ignores or is ignorant of the grim struggle waged by these men and their families until quite recent times. The fisherman may have been his own master, but he was at the mercy of wind, wave and tide, and of the capricious shoals. His was the precarious life of the hunter, surviving into an urban and industrialized society. Whatever hardships the neighbouring agricultural villages experienced, they did not compare with those of fishing communities. The risks of his life and the near-impossibility of improving his financial position made the fisherman an object of mingled pity and scorn. As Stephen Reynolds showed in his great book *A Poor Man's House* (1903), no farmer would willingly allow his daughter to marry a fisherman. Reynolds—a remarkable man, son of a gentleman of Devizes—had himself taken up a fisherman's life; and though he operated from Sidmouth beach the conditions that he so vividly depicted applied equally to Beer and to all other Devon fishing villages.

Beer did not in fact become a civil parish until 1894 or an

ecclesiastical parish until 1905, but the settlement itself is older than fishing villages commonly are. It is most picturesque, huddled close in its little valley and fronted by a small bay. Like several other places on the Devon coast it is said to have a Spanish connection. The story is basically the same whatever the setting: a village depopulated by plague; a wrecked Spanish ship (often an Armada vessel); the survivors of the storm then intermarry with the survivors of the pestilence. The physical characteristics— 'dark, broad-headed, stalwart men'—that have given rise to this legend are more satisfactorily explained as being due to the survival in these isolated places of pre-Saxon lineaments expressive of a Mediterranean immigration in the early Bronze Age. Just as romantic in fact as the legend!

What *is* remarkable here is the proven existence of smugglers' caves. Beer Head has excellent facilities for landing and storing contraband, and one of the most famous of all smugglers made use of them. Jack Rattenbury, who was born in 1778, published his *Memoirs of a Smuggler* in 1837 and revealed a good many of his secrets. By that time he had been forced by gout to retire from smuggling. Much of his success had been due to the Beer caves, his own incomparable knowledge of his native land, and the hauntings traditionally associated with Bovey House and the lane leading to it. Spirits of all kinds are the smuggler's friend.

The quarries from which the famous Beer stone came lie to the west of the village. The Old Quarry—south of the road—was worked in Roman Britain and right down to the end of the nineteenth century. It is perhaps better described as a mine rather than a quarry, for it is all underground. So, too, is the New Quarry on the other side of the road. Opened as late as 1883, it is as large as the other, yet its product seems to have been solely for restorations. From this spot came the stone out of which beauty was created all over Devon—yes, and far beyond the county's limits. It is delightful to see that Beer itself took some share of its own great building material. Cob and thatch are much in evidence, but there are also many notable examples of mellow seventeenth-century stone houses.

If you could travel like the jackdaws that haunt these cliffs, Branscombe would be only two miles and a few minutes west of Beer; and there is, indeed, a fine walk up over the headland and

down into Branscombe. But vehicles must travel by a less direct
route. Quite apart from its own distinctive loveliness, Branscombe
must be visited, for it illustrates a facet of Devon village history.
Some deny that there is a village here at all. There is, but it is non-
nucleated, straggling up its drawn-out combe.

The name means 'Brannoc's valley'; and Brannoc is a Celtic
name. The church is dedicated to St Winifred; and she was a
North Welsh saint. So, before the Saxons came the Celts were
settled here, and, though the Saxons prized the place—it was
royal property in 857 and was a named bequest in King Alfred's
will—they did nothing to change its ground-plan. The topography
would have made it hard for them to do so had they tried. Up on
the cliff edge there are Bronze Age Barrows and an Iron Age fortress. In the church itself is represented every major period of
architecture, starting with Saxon 'herring-bone' work. Thus, for
at least 2,500 years men have made their homes in and around
this tiny gap in the high cliffs. Not only the church, but the houses
fronting it and the lonely bartons straggling into the hills, speak
still of men who made their mark on local and national history.
Edge Barton was the home of the Branscombes from the Norman
Conquest until the reign of Edward III. Three sheriffs of Devon
were born here; and Walter, Bishop of Exeter from 1258 to 1280.
He lies now in justified pomp in the Lady Chapel that he built.
Never did bishop order his tomb more magnificently. Nor was it
only in his superb cathedral that his masterly hand was at work.
His native St Winifred's, here in Branscombe, and Ottery St Mary's
wonderful church responded to his touch.

After the Branscombes, the Wadhams came to Edge. Here, Dame
Dorothy retired after the death of her husband, Sir Nicholas, and
—at the age of 75—set about the immense task of administering
those terms of his will that provided for the foundation of the
Oxford college that bears the family name: and saw the work
done in a little over three years.

Church Living with its thirteenth-century features: Hole of the
Holcombes; Lower House of the Fords; Berry Barton, second of
two houses there, the earlier having been haunted by what was
quite clearly a Welsh ghost; Margel's Cottage with its oak ceil-
ing; Barnells built by Nelson's Captain of Marines on the
Victory. . . . Is there any wonder that W. H. Hudson declared that

Branscombe "had everything he wanted and had come to seek?"
It is a thought that will be echoed by most visitors. But try to get
there in the spring or the autumn; and to give yourself time to
explore. Both Branscombe and Beer make an immediate and vivid
impact, but standing and staring will bring a richer reward.

The settlements west of Branscombe emphasise the East Devon
valley pattern. Along the Sid and the Otter they string out from
the A30 to the coast and the general tendency is a north-south
run of villages with isolated farms in between. Farway is an
exception. It is tucked away in a deep hollow where the east-flow-
ing Coly cuts through the greensand heights. Up on Broad Down
there is an astonishing cluster of Bronze Age barrows—more
impressive, it has been claimed, than any such group outside
Dartmoor—and past the barrows and following the high ground
runs the ancient trackway from which the village took its name:
faer-weg or 'frequented road'. There is little traffic along it now
and Farway itself is a tiny place, distinguished chiefly for its site
and for the impressive Prideaux monuments in St Michael's church.
Sir Edmund was an eloquent pleader in the reigns of Elizabeth
and James and his stone robes sit well on his sculptured figure.
Nearby is the stone house that he built in 1607: Netherton Hall.

Another barrow-crowned height, Gittisham Hill, interposes its
long length between Farway and the road the Romans built to link
Isca with civilized Britain. West of the hill lies Gittisham itself.
(Like many a Devon village, it doesn't sound as it looks: the name
is pronounced 'Gitsam'.) It must be one of the prettiest villages
in the county. Cob and thatch predominate and the church has a
remarkably attractive interior: box-pews, a west gallery and
plenty of colour, especially on the Beaumont and Putt monuments.
Any lover of good cider should visit this place. One of the finest
apples that went into the late making—Tom Putt—was bred here
by Thomas Putt, a barrister. He also planted the fine Beech Walk
on the hill.

It's a lovely road here along the top. 'The Hare and Hounds'
stands almost at the highest point, and, when you can tear yourself away, the route drops down, slowly at first, then with gather-
ing speed, to lead you to Sidbury, where, the experts all agree, is
one of Devon's most fascinating churches. It was not until 1898
when the chancel was being restored that the Saxon crypt was

discovered. Since the spire was added in 1895, the various buildings and rebuildings thus cover a span of about a thousand years.

South-west of the village stands Sidbury Castle, an Iron Age
fort. Sand Barton, a mile to the north-east was first mentioned in
1175. Sidford's Porch House dates from 1574 and was one of
Charles II's many hiding places when he was on the run. Add to
all these some excellent pubs, stupendous views from the hilltops
around (on one of which, Roncombe Gate, the smugglers from
Salcombe, Branscombe and Beer used to rendezvous) and the
attractions of the Sid Valley villages are perhaps adequately hinted
at. Any attempt at detailed description must fail. Visit any of
them once and you will return again and again.

Whether the Sid or the Otter deserves the palm must be left
to partisans to decide. Though each is in many ways typical of
East Devon they are very different. The Otter is a broader valley
and dominated in its middle course by the beautiful town of
Ottery St Mary. It seems to me that the villages for a mile or two
around are passage ways to and from that lovely old place. Alfing-
ton (*not* to be confused with Al*ph*ington, which is now linked with
Exeter, though retaining village features: but the name's the same,
basically—'Aelfa's farm'), Tipton St John's and Harpford should
all be seen for each has noteworthy features. Yet, inevitably, they
are overshadowed by Coleridge's beautiful birthplace.

Lower down the Otter, Newton Poppleford must not be missed.
It's a big village with characteristic cob and thatch—the farther
west you go, the less the flint shows. Colaton Raleigh, to the
south, is even more the 'characteristic Devon village'—at least
as the tourist sees it. Whitewashed cob—both Devon and Somerset tend to spring clean outside as well as in!—shady trees. Many
a camera shutter has clicked there.

East Budleigh is lovely in its own right. A charming church and
a pulpit that I love because it was the work of Henry ('Harry')
Hems of Exeter. He had the endearing habit of carving his own
name bigger than the name of his subject. (Many a quick-reading
visitor to Tiverton, for example, imagines that the statue of
Edward VII, down by Lowman Green and known to aged inhabitants as 'The Peacemaker', is a statue of Harry Hems, because he
carved his name in huge letters on the plinth. What a marvellous
idea—Harry Hems, imperially bearded, wearing royal robes and

bearing sceptre in one hand and orb in the other. Oh, happy Harry Hems!)

For the romantic traveller, East Budleigh will attract as the gateway to Hayes Barton, where Sir Walter Raleigh was born. Then, if so given, you can trace him out to the beach at Budleigh Salterton (a town, not a village) and get really 'sent' by "The Boyhood of Raleigh". I often think that the romanticizers would do better to muse on his last thoughts:

> Even such is time, that takes in trust
> Our youth, our joys, and all we have,
> And pays us but with age and dust,
> Who in the dark and silent grave,
> When we have wandered all our ways,
> Shuts up the story of our days.
> And from which earth, and grave, and dust,
> The Lord shall raise me up, I trust.

He wrote that night before he was executed. It was found in his Bible in the gatehouse at Westminster. It means more than all the sloppy sentimentalizing that fools have accreted round his memory.

Otterton, very near the river's mouth, is a delightful mixture of the traditional cob and thatch and red sandstone buildings that indicate that we are on the fringes of the Exe Basin. There are several very early seventeenth-century buildings here. There is a good—a very good—early seventeenth-century building in the main street and, though the church of St Michael got clobbered by the Victorian restorers in 1871, there's enough left to suggest 'the beauty been'.

And, of course, in the parish there is Ladram Bay, one of the 'red' sections of the coast, its crumbling sandstone yielding so perceptibly to the sea that the observer who allows but two years to intervene between successive visits may easily notice the changes that the hungry waves and wandering winds are carving in the rock face.

West of the Otter the Woodbury hills rear their bold bulk. Slanting down to the lee is Woodbury itself. It takes its name from an earthworks on the summit of the ridge just to the east of the village. This fort must once have been of great strategic importance, for an ancient ridgeway passes through it and it commands the mouth of the Exe. It was not only in Iron Age times, either, that it was recognized as being a crucial spot. It was garrisoned again during the Napoleonic Wars.

Woodbury itself is the perfect Saxon nucleated defensive East Devon settlement. It was once a royal manor and was clearly a key point in the Saxon settlement programme.

The parish church (St Swithin) contains a very nasty bit of Victoriana (as well, thank goodness, as many lovely things). In 1846 the Reverend J. Loveband Fulford got the living and the pompous ass carved out chunks of the medieval rood screen so that the congregation could see him better. What possible good he thought that could do, we can only guess. He seems to have been typical of the general run of disastrous Victorian squarsons who did so much damage in Devon and whose spiritual and lay descendants continue the abominable work. Loveband Fulford did terrible things to this church. Nearby Nutwell Court, which once belonged to the Drakes, is another example of misguided 'improvements'. Fortunately, the restorers stopped work here in about 1756, so the final result is by no means as horrible as in the church.

But Woodbury, interesting as it is, must be seen principally as the termination of East Devon. Below, the marvellous 'Red Lands' open out.

3

The Exe Basin

I T is a funnel-shaped land with two lateral extensions: eastward, up the Culm valley as far as Uffculme; and westward, up the Creedy. An errant tongue of sandstone also licks out towards Hatherleigh. In a county that elsewhere—apart from the South Hams—is notable for hard farming, this is a zone of astonishing fecundity.

Those evocative authors of *Southwest England* call this 'Red Devon' and describe it as extending from Tiverton southwards to the coast. This, they say, is the 'Heartland of Devon', making clear in this vivid phrase how much the red Permian rocks have contributed to the wealth and civilization of the county. The middle and lower Exe, much of the Clyst, the Creedy and the Culm valleys constitute the chief Red Land area. And it is along these rivers that run the routes converging on Exeter—capital city of and key to Devon.

Here, on easily-worked soil, arable vies with mixed and dairy farming. Here, the farms are larger than is common in this county of small, family-run holdings. In the west, where hilly land swells up and marks the Culm Measure country, plough averages only about one-seventh of the total farm land. In some parishes in the Red Lands half is ploughed. (Though whether this will survive E.E.C. entry remains to be seen.) The best swedes in Britain are grown here at present; a red land speciality, the soil producing a flavour that makes this crop readily marketable in London, the Midlands and the North. Some wheat is grown throughout the area, though barley is the chief cereal. Friesians now, alas, pre-

dominate on the rich grazing, but there are Channel Island and
Ayrshire cattle, too; and here and there a herd of incomparable
South Devons. There is no better grass in England than is grown
in the basin of the Exe.

If Woodbury is an outlier of East Devon—as we have taken it
to be—then Topsham is the estuary head, standing partly on the
bank of the Exe and partly on an isthmus between the great river
and its tributary, the Clyst: a water that so long delays its homage
that it preserves an independent existence until the Exe itself has
broadened out into the strongly-flowing tides. Topsham cannot
claim space in this book. Its population takes it out of village
class. Nobody in his senses would lay down a figure for maximum
or minimum village population. Not, that is, as a dogmatic
absolute. Yet there is virtue in the stipulation of the recently-in-
stituted Haig Village Cricket Competition—to qualify as a village
in the terms of that contest a settlement must not exceed 2,500.
Topsham goes way above that number. Yet what a centre from
which to explore the villages of the lower basin! Steeped in
beauty and history. Replete with admirable pubs and colourful
characters.

Within easy reach is Lympstone, where a recent purchaser of
the post office discovered with some surprise that a river mooring
'went with' his property. That is typical of the place. A local
boat still brings in a catch of fish for sale in the village. The life
of Lympstone is inseparable from the waters. It is an ancient
settlement. The place-name experts cannot agree on the deriva-
tion, but it seems certain that the first element is a personal name.
The dispute turns on whether it is Celtic or an Anglo-Saxon name.
If you are looking for antiquity, the church is disappointing; but
the sandstone cliffs at the water's edge, the views across the estuary, and characteristic tidal-river smell, the period pieces dating
from the 'discovery' of Lympstone in the early nineteenth century
and—above all—the sailing, give pleasure to its inhabitants and
to its many visitors.

Between Topsham and Lympstone the traveller must pass
through Ebford and Exton—both in fact stand up remarkably well
to the traffic—and, if he is wise, he will bear left-handed to Clyst
St George. There are six parishes that take their names from the

Clyst river and this is the last of them. Its church has suffered more vicissitudes than most. The Victorians rebuilt it and ruined it. The Germans burnt it out in 1940. It has sprung up again; the phoenix should not be ignored. In any case, it is on the way to Woodbury Salterton where those indispensable men, the salt workers, used to live. Down on the coast at Budleigh the salt was obtained from sea-water evaporated in salt pans. Here, on a stream, well above high water, it was probably mineral. Littleham, a few miles south, was once, as its name tells us, a very rural spot indeed. Now, Exmouth has almost swallowed it; but it is not without attractions. The much-restored church still attests its ancient origins and contains a splendid memorial to that sad woman, Nelson's widow, who is buried here.

On the other side of estuary, taking the bold but now afforested heights of the Haldons as the westward boundary, and John Keats' old haunts at Dawlish as the southern, there is a delightful blend of coastal and inland settlement. Brunel's great railway line follows the sea so closely as to suggest that he was dreaming of mighty steamships when he planned it. Surely as picturesque a route as any in the world. It gives Alphington— now merged with Exeter, but rural enough when Charles Dickens put his feckless parents out to grass there—a widish berth. Then it closes in on Exminster; a name that proclaims its Saxon origins. This was a key settlement when the 'Englishing' of the Exe Basin was first put in hand. The original plan is still visible despite the latter-day sprawl, and it is not altogether a surprise to discover that the first church ('minster') on this spot was in the Sherborne diocese back in 705.

South of Exminster there is a fascinating study in transport history. The railway swoops towards the coast—low and marshy here—passing within a quarter of a mile of Turf Lock, entrance to the first ship canal ever built in Britain. As the railway makes its eastward curve, the road (very close to the trains at Exminster) moves west and the two pincer in Powderham. The line is on its way to Starcross; the road is making for the same place but passes through Kenton on its way. These three features—canal, railway and road—cover four hundred years of commercial history, each linked with the rise and fall of ports and markets.

Kenton is another of the Saxon 'plantation' villages. They

tightened their grip on the Exe Basin as quickly as they could, from the very mouth of the estuary right up into the hilly land that hems it in on all sides. These big villages were, as Dogbery would have said, 'the eftest way'. Large enough to hold a work force that could exploit the rich land and, when necessary, provide an impressive body of tough infantrymen, they put the Saxon stamp on Devon's heartland. Here, the Saxon churches were built and the Saxon way of life established. Move down in one day from a village in the Exmoor foothills—Challacombe, for example—to a village in the Exe Basin: you will feel the history in your bones.

Kenton is comfortable. It is conscious of peace and plenty. Its church, one of Devon's glories, proclaims the stability with which geology and climate have blessed this land. West tower, south porch, great screen, Beer stone arcades: colour, gilding, carving, strength, light. . . . When 'foreigners' rhapsodize about Devon, singing the praises of cream and cider, their half-truths are true of the heartland.

Where the railway and the road once more come together—at Starcross—was once the river crossing for Kenton. Here are the remnants of a dream that failed, for one of Brunel's pumping stations was built here to power his 'atmospheric railway'. When it worked—when the rats left the leather valves alone—the trains glided swiftly and noiselessly to Newton Abbot. It was a brilliant and costly failure, replaced by conventional steam locomotives. There is a sense in which Starcross itself is a failure. It was hoped to develop it into a watering place, but Dawlish won. Yet, down by the river, Starcross has a kind of gentility—a little gone to seed maybe—that evokes a pleasing melancholy. Very early Victorian: rather Christmas-cardy, even in the summer. South of Starcross the river and railway and the settlements share a common story. A wooden viaduct (later replaced by a stone embankment) was built to carry the line over a two-hundred-yard stretch of the Cockwood marshes; and where the great beak of Dawlish Warren thrusts out into the estuary it was expedient to make a station for the benefit of the growing number of visitors. Visually not the most attractive bit of Devon, this stretch of coast and its villages have a good deal of industrial archaeology to show and social history to teach.

Inland again, and at the foot of the Haldons, Kenn and Kenn-

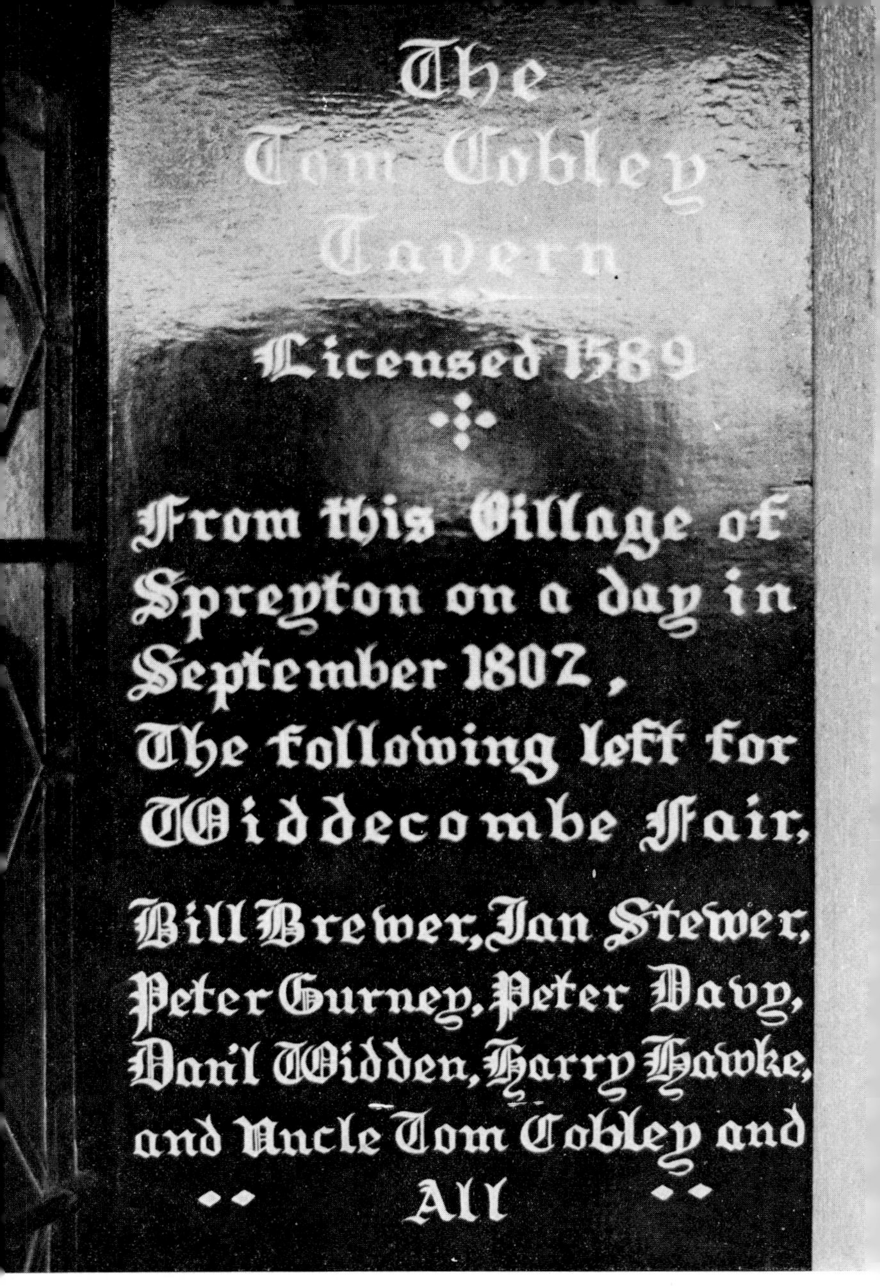

The Tom Cobley Tavern

Licensed 1589

❖

From this Village of
Spreyton on a day in
September 1802 ,
The following left for
Widdecombe Fair,

Bill Brewer, Jan Stewer,
Peter Gurney, Peter Davy,
Dan'l Widden, Harry Hawke,
and Uncle Tom Cobley and
All

Immortals at Spreyton

A thatcher's tools at Sampford Courtenay

All Saints, Holbeton

The 'Exeter Inn' at Modbury

ford offer the more usual and more satisfying sights. Kenn stands
on fine sandstone and though there is a lot of alien softwood up
on the hills, there is still a good deal of noble native timber in the
parish. (Devon, incidentally, is as a whole by no means as well-
wooded a county as is supposed. The more reason then to praise
the County Council's imaginative 'plant a tree' campaign.) The
trees and the splendid farms of Kenn provide a fine backcloth for
St Andrew's—superbly sited and deep red in colour, as befits a
Red Land church. Its building and furnishings range in period
from the early fourteenth century to 1889, when the rood was
added to the screen. It was carved in Oberammergau and is said to
be the first rood to be put into a Devon church since the Reformation. I find this fact more interesting than the rood itself; though
I am probably being insensitive! It has been much admired. Even
more interesting is the careful separation of the painted saints
on the screen panels: males to the north and females to the south.
No doubt a reminder that though matrimony is blessed by the
church in this world, there is in heaven neither giving nor taking
into that state.

Kennford is a 'street village' and a neat example of how a
route can dictate a site. A delightful spot this for a summer's day
drink while the traffic thunders along the A38 and we natives can
stretch our legs and take our ease—and congratulate ourselves
on knowing the back lanes.

North-east of Exeter there is hilly ground; a big bluff that overlooks the fertile valley and divides it from the lower Clyst. Up here
the Britons had a camp and the Romans a signal station. Leaving
the city by this quiet route you are surprisingly soon into deep
country and following a narrow, winding, up-and-down lane with
signposts that tempt you to Pinhoe and Poltimore. You pass
through Stoke Woods, where the nightingale sings, and join the
valley road at Stoke Canon.

Pinhoe itself has been absorbed by Exeter—as have, long ago,
Heavitree and St Thomas—but its church is fine and should not be
missed. It *was* a village church once. All fifteenth-century, though
its font is an interesting hybrid Saxon-Norman piece, and blush-
ing red—like the much later vicarage—it has a glorious screen.
Its best known feature is, I suppose, 'The Poor Man of Pinhoe' who

E

stands guard over the almsbox. All sorts of legends have grown round him, but the sober fact is that the manikin is the representation of a parish beadle of about 1700. Somewhere in the parish the Danes won a victory in 1001, but nobody knows quite where.

Pinhoe is a convenient gateway to a broad plain dotted with comfortable villages and spacious farms. Here and there a little place like Poltimore, its church complete with squire's pew and fireplace, has an unmistakably Georgian air, though many relics that are centuries older survive. Whimple (Celtic: 'white pool') may not be one of the visually exciting villages but it is the world-famous centre of one of Devon's best-known industries. Here Whiteways make their cider and nearly three hundred acres of orchards provide some of the fruit. They are by no means the only cider-apple orchards in the heartland. This area produces vast quantities from dozens of small orchards. But the Whimple orchards are most certainly worth a visit.

It is dangerous to declare a preference, but, in the whole of this gentle, easy-going bit of Devon, Broad Clyst must surely come high on anyone's list of favourites. It is the centre of a huge parish, shading off into higher land in the north. At least half a dozen of the farms are pre-Conquest and many of the others only just midded Domesday. The parish was remarkable for the number of its freeholders, among whom were the Churchills—Churchill Farm was recorded in Henry II's reign—ancestors of the present family.

The village itself has plenty of cob and thatch—very calendar-worthy indeed. It has a church that is believed to have been the model on which Cullompton's great 'wool' church was based. Extensive rebuilding in the late fourteenth century was probably the work of Bishop Stafford, for that most intriguing emblem, the Stafford knot, appears on one of the nave capitals. Monuments of unusual interest abound. Especially interesting are the Acland and Drewe examples, epitomising Renaissance piety—that peculiar blend of godliness tempered by humanistic values.

The parish contains so many historic houses that the explorer is spoilt for choice, but Columbjohn and Killerton must be seen. At Columbjohn before the Conquest farming went on; and by 1235 it was in the hands of John de Culm who took his name from the river and gave it to his big farm. It then passed to the Earls of

Devon and, finally, late in Elizabeth's days, to Sir John Acland who built a new house here. Here this famous Devon family lived until, in 1750 or so, they built a mansion for themselves at nearby Killerton. When they moved to the more splendid house the old one was pulled down. It seems sad that so little—the old gateway—remains of a house that was held for Charles Stuart, was Fairfax's headquarters when his army was at Silverton, and which briefly housed Cromwell himself.

Thousands of people know Killerton for its gardens, and it has indeed great charm. The Aclands lived there from the time the house was built until 1971 when Sir Richard moved out having some years previously given Killerton to the National Trust. A residential hostel of St Luke's College, Exeter, was established there some years ago, and on the summit of the wooded hill behind the house a small earthworks was built nearly 2,500 years ago.

It seems probable however, that Killerton may be remembered for a treacherous deed: the route for the Bristol-Exeter motorway, the M5, is planned to pass through the estate, and the National Trust in whose keeping it seemed safe has so far failed to convince the Ministry of the Environment that Trust property cannot be taken over.

Two of the other Clysts are of special interest. Clyst St Lawrence is well up the valley and almost into East Devon territory. It's a tiny place, yet the granite font is evidence of a church in this lonely spot since at least 1200. The present building dates from the early fifteenth century. What a period that was! The overwhelming majority of Devon's village churches date from then. Most visitors to Clyst St Lawrence will be pleased with its gargoyles and grotesques, but its most remarkable possession is the medieval painting over the chancel arch. This is said to represent the Trinity (it is by no means easy to make sense of it without that clue) and is the only one of its kind in the whole county. The other remarkable Clyst, Clyst St Mary, is very near to Exeter. Scenically, it is not distinguished; but it *does* lie at the east end of Devon's most ancient bridge and it was here that the infamous Russell finally overcame the Western Rebels and celebrated his victory by burning the village in 1549.

It is tempting to linger in Clyst country, so quiet and fruitful and unspoilt: appley, cidery, creamy, bucolic. And oh, so tempting to play that rewarding game of looking up names on the one-inch map, forming an image of what they are like, and then exploring. Listen: Jack-in-the-Green; Merry Harriers; Halfway; Hand and Pen; Budlake (straight out of Hardy it would seem but, in fact, genuine); Farthings, Wish Meadow Lane; Owleshayes; Brockhill; Black Dog . . . irresistible.

Where the Culm river joins the Exe there is a maze of water-courses, and every winter the low-lying fields are enriched by the floods. Between the two rivers, but at a bridging point of the Culm stands Stoke Canon. Here, two arms of the river must be crossed, so the bridge is a long one. And an ancient one: the recipient of a legacy in the will of Bishop Stapledon (1326). Widened to accommodate modern traffic—this is the main road from Exeter to Tiverton—it is still very narrow and often causes delays. They will do away with it, I suppose, and replace it so that the monstrous motor car can proceed unchecked. The irony is that all the way alongside this narrow, winding road there once ran one of the loveliest railways in England. Not so many years ago you could travel in civilized comfort from Exeter to Tiverton—yes, and on to Bampton and Dulverton—on the never-sufficiently-to-be-mourned Exe Valley Line. What folly to scrap it. They said it didn't 'pay'. I don't suppose it did: but the various road-widening schemes carried out since would have kept the little line open for a generation. And, with all that spent, this road is still narrow and danger-ous, with very few safe passing places in the fifteen miles between Exeter and Tiverton.

Stoke Canon used to be called Hrocastoc ('rooks' farm') but in 938 King Athelstan granted the manor to Exeter monastery, so the canons took over from the rooks. Apart from the name there is not a lot to tell the casual visitor how ancient a settlement this is, and it has been disfigured by some expensive and utterly unattractive modern building. It's handy for Exeter; but oh, those little boxes that we call houses in post-war England! Yet there are attractive old cottages and farmhouses here, their presence making the new estate the more noticeable.

The church has a tall and lovely tower and an enigmatic Nor-man font, the figures supporting the bowl of which are in danger of having their heads bitten off by four crouching beasts. There are some nice slate floor slabs celebrating local worthies, but the rebuilding of 1836 did not leave a lot behind.

On the outskirts of Stoke Canon there is a large agricultural implement depot where huge and strange-shaped red and yellow beasts—some of which look uncannily like triffids—cluster round their abestos sheds. From time to time one of them moves ponderously onto the road, breathing heavily. Next door is one of Devon's best-known cider makers. Horrells have been at Stoke Canon for a long time and they still supply a good many pubs as well as private customers. At the garage by the bridge, high up on a chimney stack, is a sign—it must go back to the twenties—advertising 'Pratts'. A nice thought to preserve it, although extensive rebuilding is taking place. Stoke Canon is very much a 'street' village, springing up at a bridging point. Its excellent garage is the twentieth-century equivalent of smithy and staging post. Its paper mill, down by the river, employs well over one hundred people and, therefore, ranks as quite a big concern in this part of the world.

Rewe, the next village up the valley, straggles rather uncertainly along the busy road, yet somehow manages to seem aloof. Apart from the church and Rewe Barton—an enormous red-brick frontage—there is nothing very noteworthy, yet the overall impression is pleasing. An especially interesting church, the interior of which will repay hours—even days—of examination; that big farm which exemplifies Red Land farming; and—a peculiarity this—a house that Brunel designed. I always call it 'the iron house'. It isn't, of course, but it looks as if it ought to be.

North of Rewe is the Ruffwell crossroads, a blessed spot. Turn east and you reach Silverton; turn west, and Thorverton welcomes you. Silverton is a copybook example of a Saxon settlement village. Surprisingly, it has been suggested that the name means 'farm by the miry ford'—a small stream rises nearby and flows into the Culm. Equally possible—and again, the topography would support the interpretation—is 'ford by the sulh or hollow'. Whichever feature most impressed the Saxons when they named it, they very soon saw it as a key spot and expanded it rapidly. Like so many others of this nature, it was in royal ownership in pre-Conquest days; and later had a market and a fair and counted as a 'borough'. The modern continuation of this bygone bustle is the paper mill which, like the mill at Hele (near Bradninch), uses raw material brought in at Watchet on the Somerset coast. Book paper is produced at the Silverton mill and a variety of high-grade papers at Hele.

Silverton is very much the centre of its large and beautiful, hilly parish. A maze of lanes, Domesday farms, red plough on hillsides, the emerald green of good Devon grass—such are the elements composing a picture of rare harmonies. The lovely church was ill treated in 1863—they took the old screen out and chopped it up—but still has much to offer. It is particularly interesting because, when most of the construction took place in the late fifteenth century, the builders made use of the volcanic stone. Up and down the Exe valley, and particularly in the bordering hills there are examples of this. At Washfield, for instance, good use was made of a quarry, dug where once, in the fiery birth pangs of the earth, a volcano spouted lava.

Silverton Park was to have been a great house. The last Earl of Egremont was at work there in 1843, when his classical-style mansion was described as 'not finished'. He died in 1845 and the house is finished now: finished off by time, neglect and Devonshire wind and rain.

But Silverton must not be left on such a note. Get into the village, admire the remarkable cob and thatch—sixteenth century right through to nineteenth—drink the beer, and walk those lanes.

Thorverton—some errant Scandinavian set up house here once—is another gem of a place. Its mill is a lovely thing and still working. It was there at Domesday (serving then, it must be confessed, the Manor of Silverton—but this one does not emphasize when visiting Thorverton!). But the fascinating feature of Thorverton—apart from the lovely little green and the tiny bridges across the stream—is the 'Dolphin' crossroads. Over and over again, this is a feature to be looked for in Devon. There is a river valley up which the main road now passes. We are so accustomed to this that we think it is the 'natural' route. It is now: has been since clearance was followed by turnpikes. It was not so once. The valley bottoms were shunned. The routes used to run over what are now side-roads. For many a century the main road from Exeter to Tiverton went 'up over'; and in those days the 'Dolphin' cross was a busy junction. It's a beautiful spot today, and the 'Dolphin' is a name to conjure with; but Thorverton is blessed in all its pubs and its cricket ground. Blessed in its church, too, where the Shepherd's Plays are enacted and there is good music, and a living community. There's that wonderful butcher's shop built in what Professor Hoskins calls 'local style' and dates at 1763. There are the excellent eighteenth- and nineteenth century houses along 'station road', leading to a station that folly has destroyed. The visitor wishing to absorb the history and atmosphere of the Exe Basin could hardly do better than base himself at either Thorverton or Silverton and then divide his time equally between the two.

Or should he perhaps choose Bradninch? East of Silverton, tucked away where the hills fold above the Culm, this 'decayed borough and market town' proclaims its long history not only in its own visible relics but in the perpetuation of its ancient honourable name in the county town's streets, squares and buildings. The Earl of Cornwall used to hold Bradninch as a barony and it was a natural son (obviously, legitimate heirs are 'unnatural'?) of Henry I who granted 'the town' its first charter. Thirty years or so later King John gave to Bradninch "all such liberties and free customs" as Exeter itself enjoyed. A Thursday market and a three-day fair followed. 1337 saw Bradninch finally swallowed into the Duchy of Cornwall. It is still Duchy owned.

Between James I's reign and 1835 Bradninch was a borough. Perhaps it was not unreasonable to remove it from the roll, for its councillors were spending half its income in feasting themselves. (That was a much better record than most Devon boroughs could show.) Reasonable or not, the status was removed and by that day the woollen and lace manufacture had also gone. Even the weekly market was a mere memory. But for the Hele paper mills, Bradninch would have sunk to nothing. It is worth remembering that it was at these mills that the first glazed writing paper in all Britain was produced, and that this rural spot manufactured the paper that was used for the catalogues of the Great Exhibition in 1851.

It is really a wonder that any cob and thatch village in Devon has survived. The materials were vulnerable to fire—to weather, too, if 'hat' or 'shoes' were neglected—and hardly one of these venerable settlements has escaped unscathed. Bradninch is no exception. A series of fires gutted most of the old buildings. And even the church, though spared by fire, was gutted by man in the mid-nineteenth century. Restoring zeal did spare the lovely rood screen. And—unusually—there is another screen across the tower arch. The church has an unusual dedication, too: St Dionysius. Perhaps that had something to do with the fires. Under Castle Hill there is a manor house looking much more eighteenth- than mid-fifteenth-century—which was when it was originally built. Its interior is remarkable for woodwork and ceilings, the comparison being—as, in Devon, it always must be—with Bradfield, near Willand.

Over the hills behind Bradninch there are lovely walks to Tiverton through little-visited Butterleigh, and from there down the Burn river and back that way into the Exe valley; or, as many would prefer, down to Bickleigh, one of Devon's most photographed spots. Few visitors bother with the church, high up over the bridge. It has some of the finest monuments and the most moving epitaphs in the whole of Devon. Like all other villages in this valley, Bickleigh is now choked with summer traffic. I remember going to a farm wedding there years ago—I don't remember coming away—where the celebratory drink was tumblers-full of whisky. The road was quiet enough then for my homeward-bound and erratic bicycle to carry me safely. Nowadays, you are not safe on the A396 with more than a pint of what passes for beer inside you.

Tiverton, 'the town of the two fords', opens up the Exe route to Bampton, along which Bolham and Cove mark the winding river-road. There is a celebrated 'meeting house' at Bolham, and a pillar of Congregationalism told me once, just after he had put through a very advantageous property deal, that he found it easier "to meet the Lord" in Bolham than anywhere else in Devon. I can't say that I have shared his experience. Bampton, of course, everyone knows for its castle—though there is very little left of it—and for its great autumnal fair. Its castle played quite a part in the troubled events of Stephen's reign, mostly because that hard-drinking glutton Robert of Bampton was in possession of property which the Abbot of Glastonbury (Stephen's brother) claimed. The property chiefly in dispute was the manor of Uffculme, and the tangled and fascinating story goes back before the Conquest. There is no space to tell it here—though we should not pass through Bampton without remembering the unfortunate archer taken and hanged to bring about surrender of the fortress.

Apart from the Exmoor pony fair there is little to suggest that Bampton was one a market 'town' and active in the wool trade. It has a wide and pleasant main street with one or two well-looking houses, some beautiful roses, a quarry that from time to time hits veins of the loveliest stone in Devon, the 'White Horse', and a quiet little church, upon the tower of which the traveller looks down if he comes in from the north.

If you go due north of Bampton, up over the hills, you don't stay in Devon for long. It's stretching a topographical point, I think, but we might as well agree that the Exe Basin ends at Exbridge. Certainly, the Exe river changes character here, for it picks up the Barle as a tributary and ceases at this point to be known as 'the Little Exe'. Exbridge, just in Devon, is hardly a village, but since it is the county's end it would be improper to ignore it. It would also be ungrateful, for it is the home of Bill Gunter, a craftsman of great skill (the Gunter family have been builders here for a long time) John Panton's nationally-known nursery garden, and the 'Anchor', one of the best inns in all Devon. Not a bad ending!

This last stretch of the Exe Basin, starts, as we have seen, at Tiverton. But that busy town is also the gateway to an eastern plain through which the A373 travels to join that overburdened A38, and through which 'the bumper' used to run to 'Tivvy Junc'. Halberton was once important enough to give its name to a hundred. The church is very fine indeed. Good judges have claimed that its rood screen is unequalled in all England. Halberton Pond, however, is probably the village's most remarkable feature. Fed by warm springs, it has never frozen. The former Grand Western Canal passes through the parish and now that the whole eleven-mile stretch (from Tiverton to Greenham) is to become a linear country park (under the terms of the Countryside Act of 1968) it is likely that Halberton will become known again. There is rich land in the parish and some of the Domesday farms are very large and thriving. This, like the rest of the basin, is an exceptional area of Devon, where poor farmers are as rare as dead donkeys.

Halberton's sister village, Sampford Peverell, is on the edge of hillier land. Much decayed from its 'borough' days, it has picturesque features and was one of the several places round here where John Wesley fought a notable battle with a poltergeist. He stilled the troublesome 'elemental' but it flared up again in the nineteenth century. Look out for 'The Ghost House'.

"Burlescombe for stones: Holcombe for hones"—so the old saying ran. The Burlescombe bit is easy to interpret. There are important quarries here or, rather, at Westleigh in the parish. The church had much love and money lavished on it in the fifteenth century and is surely one of the most colourful of our parish churches to this day, the Ayshford monuments being particularly lovely.

The 'hones' of Holcombe must refer to the sharpening tools so much in use in a village that had a long tradition of furniture making. Most of it was carried out in tiny 'garden shed workshops'. Holcombe Court—home of the Bluetts for four hundred years— has been described as "the finest Tudor house in Devon". It really is a most lovely building, its hall and three-storied tower porch being its finest features. My own favourite memories of Holcombe Rogus centre on the church: the view from the top of the tower, the exquisite and deeply moving Bluett monuments in the north chapel, the early sixteenth-century church house.

Marking a precise western boundary between the Exe Basin and Mid-Devon is not always easy, and particular difficulty arises just north of Exeter. The Creedy valley, certainly as far as Crediton, must be seen as belonging to the heartland. Newton St Cyres— 'the new farm whose church is dedicated to St Ciricius'—is as attractive a village as Devon has to show: and I sometimes think that nowhere in the county does the Devon tongue ring more truly. The church—its 'modern' dedication is to St Julitta and St St Cyriac—is early fifteenth-century with a lot of seventeenth-century woodwork. However, the twentieth century can happily claim some credit for its present beauty, the restoration having been delayed until the early years of this age (1914–21) and then carried out with deep feeling for the total effect. Old Devon families—the Quickes and the Northcotes—have done what they could to achieve immortality by building their monuments over the centuries. The Northcote memorials are of particular interest, for they record how the family made a fortune in wool (at Crediton), consolidated it by marriage (to a Drewe) and invested it in land (all around). The village itself makes a pretty cluster of colour-washed cob and thatch round the church.

Beyond Crediton, about as far as it is safe to go in a chapter devoted to the Exe Basin, lies that lovely village of Sandford noteworthy for its cottages and for the fine houses scattered about the parish. Carews and Davies (land and wool again) abound. Bremridges were here for five hundred years, and Ruxford Barton first went on record in a charter dated 930, when the canons of Crediton became by pious gift the largest landowners in the parish. What do they know of Devon who only Torquay know?

Upton Hellions is a parish without a village but deserves attention because of its name. Upton: 'the *tun*' (settlement) further up than Crediton. Hellions: a manor held in 1242 by William de Helihun, a Breton name. The old migration in reverse!

A slightly crooked line may be given to the boundary here. Bring Cheriton Fitzpaine into the heartland, then curve firmly back to the B3214 and follow its ups and downs to Bickleigh's lovely bridge. Further west we cannot go. Cheriton means 'church farm' and the settlement went to a shareholder in Norman William's successful take-over in 1066. (I'm never quite happy about the Norman victory.) There was settlement, civilization and a church here before the Normans dispossessed the Saxons. It is a big and delightful village with some fine memorials in its prosperous-looking church. Upcott Barton was the scene of a nasty bit of Wild West thuggery in the mid-fifteenth century. Nicholas Radford, a lawyer, was murdered by Thomas, son of the Earl of Devon, and the estate then passed into Courtenay hands. One can share Dr Johnson's opinions of 'attorneys' and yet feel that poor Nicholas Radford was badly treated.

Due south is Stockleigh Pomeroy, sister village of Stockleigh English. Stockleigh is 'the farm in the clearing'—the names indicate that we are on the very borders of our territory—and Gilebertus and Anglicus held one manor in 1242, having been preceded by Henry de la Pumerai in possession of the other. In both cases the little settlements are remarkable chiefly as being outposts of Red Land Devon, richly based, but very near the heavy soil. The nearby Raddon Hills command extensive views of what most 'foreigners' would call typical Devon.

Shobrooke ('sheep brook') lies more securely within the frontier. A smiling land of peace and plenty, where minor gentry and substantial yeomen used to flourish. The church was messed about in a late Victorian frenzy, but they left the Norman doorway which is made of Thorverton stone. (That splended village never of course rivalled Beer, but its limited output was of excellent quality.) Thomas Westcote wrote his *View of Devonshire* at West Raddon, in Shobrooke parish—a sufficient reason for a pilgrimage.

The village of Cadbury had not been begun when Cadbury Castle was constructed high upon its hilltop. Some have held that the views from here are the most extensive in Devon. Dartmoor and Exmoor seem within spitting distance. The Quantocks and Bodmin Moor can be seen. In the lee of the great Iron Age fort 'Cada's *burh*' grew—'ripened' would be a better word—to perfection Only one sad thing here: a few of the old bench-ends remain in the church to show what was lost when the restorers got to work in about 1860. It would almost be better not to know. But no regrets can be allowed to spoil Cadbury.

The circle has been completed: we are back at Bickleigh. The 'castle'—Saxon work has been found in the grounds—was never a castle really, but it was a moated manor house, itself built where older fortifications stood. In its time it belonged to the Courtenays and to the Carews. Carews were the rectors of Bickleigh for about three hundred years and the son of one of them achieved a fame that the family felt it could do without. Bampfylde Moore Carew (1690–1758) was an early example of a drop-out. He became a gipsy; lived a rogue's life (and told some merry tales about it); was transported to the American colonies; escaped to England; was 'up' with Bonny Prince Charlie and had the sense not to turn back at Derby, but made for Bickleigh like a homing pigeon. He died there peacefully with the sound of the Exe to speed him on his way.

4

Torbay

A T the northern foot of Great Haldon the A38 branches. Spectacular engineering has taken place here. Its southern spur—the A380—climbs the once-notorious Telegraph Hill on its way to Newton Abbot and Totnes. The northern road—the A38 itself—curves round Dartmoor on its way to Plymouth. The A380 thus forms the western extremity of the sub-region that is called Torbay (not, of course, to be confused with the administrative area at present so named). The northern limit of the sub-region is marked by the course of the Dawlish water: the southern limit is formed by the Dart river from Dartington down to the sea. The area between the two roads shares some characteristics common to both the Torbay and the Dartmoor sub-zones.

Although there is much fine countryside in this zone and some of the best farming land outside the Exe Basin, the area is unique in being the one part of Devon to have lost its predominantly rural feel. Neither Exeter nor Plymouth so forcefully asserts an urbanizing influence as does the great arc of 'resort land' that sprawls along the once-lovely coast. To many that must seem a harsh judgement, and there are mitigating factors that must in fairness be mentioned.

There are still a few quiet and secret places, even on the coast itself, particularly at its extremities: between Dawlish and Teignmouth; north of Torquay; flanking Brixham. Again, much depends upon the time of year. I would not willingly enter this zone of Devon during 'the season' for it is then that the coastal pressure surges inland, choking the lanes and destroying the peace while—

and this must not be forgotten—bringing some useful money into the rural economy. Out of season, however, inland Torbay has much to offer.

There is a good deal of red land, but the area is more varied, topographically, than the Exe Basin. The afforested gravels of Haldon contrast markedly with the Devonian limestones that form the two arms of Tor Bay itself. South of the Teign estuary, red Permian rocks shade off into sandstones, grits and shales. Red land outcrops again round Paignton and spreads inland carrying its richness with it; but in the broad Bovey Basin there is a fair amount of heath. This is a rolling landscape, not plentifully wooded, except in the Dart valley. Mixed farming predominates; the villages are nucleated; cob and thatch are the native building materials. The climate is mild. The land is fertile. There are pockets of specialized horticulture and fruit growing. It is not the best of Devon simply because for so many people it has become the best-known part of Devon.

In the spring of 1818, when Dawlish was in its infancy as a 'watering place', John Keats and his brother Tom were staying at Teignmouth. They were unlucky with the weather, a doubly unfortunate circumstance since Tom had come as a very sick man and the hope had been that Devon's kind airs would be good for his 'consumption'. It rained so hard and so often during their three weeks' stay that John described the land as "a country under hatches" and wrote exasperatedly:

You may say what you will of Devonshire: the truth is, it is a splashy, rainy, misty, snowy, foggy, haily, floody, muddy, slipshod county. The hills are very beautiful, when you get sight of 'em; the primroses are out, but you are in; the cliffs are of a fine deep colour, but then the clouds are continually vying with them. . . . The flowers here wait as naturally for the rain twice a day as mussels do for the tide. This Devonshire is like Lydia Languish, very entertaining when it smiles, but cursedly subject to sympathetic moisture.

Fortunately, it didn't rain every day. On the six fine days they were allowed, Keats rambled delightedly through the lanes and villages along the Teign and over the Little Haldon hills into Dawlish. All patriotic Devonians will prefer to regard his light-

hearted occasional verses as a truer description than the prose
just quoted.

> Here all the summer could I stay,
>   For there's Bishop's teign
>   And King's teign
> And Coomb at the clear teign head—
>   Where close by the stream
>   You may have your cream
> All spread upon Barley bread.

That is a fair sample of the happy doggerel that he enclosed in his
letters when Devonshire was pleasing him. If at other times he
wrote differently—though usually with humour—we have to remember that Tom Keats urgently needed sunshine and that their
small resources were being strained to keep him in lodgings for the
sake of the warm air so unkindly denied him.

The villages named in his rhymes have changed. Kingsteignton
has now gone well above the population limit adopted—flexibly,
I hope—as part of the village definition used in this book. It is a
long and depressing place. There is little of the native style to be
seen in the buildings, the material for which has been—it appears
—hastily assembled and in response to urgent needs. The *patience*
of cob and thatch is what one misses. But the place has had its
history. It was founded very early in the Saxon settlement—'the
king's *tun* on the Teign'—and it has continuing vitality: there
are modern potteries here, using the local clay.

Nearby Bishopsteignton retains its village feel. It is the principal
settlement in a large parish and belonged to the bishops of Exeter
before the Normans came. In fact, at Redway—'the Red Way'—
there was a summer palace for these bishops, though there isn't
a lot left now, except the 'gothic' lettering on the Ordnance Map.
Architecturally, Bishopsteignton is distinguished for its pleasant
'Regency' buildings; cool, elegant and white. Most of those would
have been new, or unbuilt, when Keats went that way. He certainly enjoyed the splendid views over the estuary and inland towards Little Haldon. This, in fact, was a route that he took:

> Over the Hill and over the Dale,
> And over the Bourne to Dawlish

—following the ancient trackway past Lindbridge ('Limetree ridge'?) which a Barbados merchant built in 1673, and on to Luton ('Leofwynn's farm'), there turning left for Ideford instead of taking the direct way to Dawlish. He could hardly resist this lovely little bowl in the hills, where a tiny and over-restored church yet retains a fragment of its Norman predecessor.

In a similarly secluded spot stands Ashcombe, with a small church, the dedication of which (St Necton) indicates a continuing history since the fifth century. Ashcombe has been very lucky. Restoration was early here (1824–5) and was most beautifully done. Such a lot of lovely colour and fine carving; some of the latter old, some belonging to the early nineteenth century yet exactly in the spirit of the older workmen.

It is cheating to include Mamhead, for there is a parish, some farms and a great house, but no true village. Yet anyone taking the mazy way from Ashcombe round and back to Dawlish is bound to notice the trees and the obelisk and to be curious. The estate has been owned by a succession of merchants, one of whom— Thomas Ball—brought back from his adventurous journeys the many exotic trees now in the park. He also built the obelisk "out of regard to the safety of such as might use to sail out of the Port of Exon or any others who might be driven on the coast". The church stands in the park—so does an Iron Age fort—and Arch-bishop Frederick Temple's grandfather was rector here. He was a friend of James Boswell's and the story is told that he persuaded Boswell to take a vow to lead an abstemious life. The promise was made at the great churchyard yew. The tree lived on, though the oath-taker was forsworn.

Newton Abbot occupies a lot of space on the south bank of the river but is flanked by some very pretty villages. Up the valley, Teigngrace must allure by the sound of its name alone. As so often happens, the modern form and sound are misleading: the manor was known quite straightforwardly as Taigna or Tengue until it became the possession of a family called de la Bruere. It then changed to Teygne Bruere or Teynghebruer. The 'grace' replaced the 'bruer' when it passed into the hands of Geoffrey Gras. So the name means 'the Teign manor belonging to Geoffrey the fat one'. But don't be put off. There is a great deal to see in the church, of

unusual nineteenth-century interest. Stover House, now a girls'
school, was the home of the Templers, who took a patrician and
benevolent interest in their village, building the present church,
making a canal—to transport the ball clay—and (in 1820) con-
structing one of the early tramways. George Templer then owned
Hay Tor quarries, and for forty years quarry stone was trundled
down the granite rails to the canal quay.

East of Newton, along the estuary shore, old farms, houses and
villages straggle in very Devonshire fashion. Haccombe-with-
Combe is a very large parish, created when two ancient parishes
were joined. A long valley runs down to the river: at its head,
appropriately, stands Combeinteignhead; at its foot stands
'Coombe Cellars'. Thousands of visitors will have pleasant memories of the inn. It does a roaring trade in the season—and deserves
to. This is a quiet enough spot on a winter's night. Just the long
saltings and the sound of the wind—and, how pleasant to be able
to stress the word, *genuine* memories of smugglers. Look first at
the map to see why it was such a good centre for the free trade.
Then visit the place and use your eyes. The natural advantages are
obvious. Another interesting point is that the free traders flourished here in the early nineteenth century, a little after the general
heyday. Of course, we romanticise the 'old-fashioned' smuggling.
"Brandy for the parson, baccy for the clerk" sounds so harmless.
It was usually brutal, sordid and ruthless, however much we may
feel that excise duties were—and remain—an unnatural imposi-
tion.

Back in Combe itself, the Bourchier almshouses are quietly pleasing. The foundation date, 1620, is a guarantee of that. (So is the
material—red sandstone.) I wonder why it was, or what it was,
that inspired men to build so beautifully then? There is no sense
of effort here. No self-conscious flourishes or effect-seeking. The
façade does not attempt to impress. Perhaps that is the answer to
my question. In the church the Hockmores of nearby Buckland
Barton flout oblivion with their monuments. Alice, who died in
1613, has the most impressive tomb in the church. And that, when
you think of it, is interesting. These same people who could build
with such quiet dignity were not reluctant to trim up their graves.
Symbols, epitaphs, expensive materials, sculpture, brasses . . . they
used them all. I think they got away with it because they were less

F

concerned with an egotistic aggrandisement—though that plays a part—than with conquering the universal conqueror, Death. The ostentation of the monuments is an attempt to remove the sting from life's ultimate insult: extinction. For the Hockmores, inhabitants of Buckland Barton for so many generations, death must have been especially galling. To be wrenched away from so delectable a life!

Haccombe itself is inland from Combe and consists of little more than the mansion and the church. The manor descended from Haccombes to Courtenays to Carews.

If Combe church can boast some supreme bench-ends Haccombes's St Blaize is known throughout the world for its effigies, and brasses and monuments. 'Important', 'remarkable', 'the best in Devon'—those are merely a sample of the experts' eulogies. Haccombes, Courtenays and Carews: there they lie. "Man is a noble animal, splendid in ashes, and pompous in the grave." No student of history or of human nature can neglect Haccombe.

Deep in another valley, though linked with Combe, Stokeinteignhead was observed by Leland in Henry VIII's reign to be "no great thing". We can accept the factual basis of the comment while rejecting the dismissive note. It's a relief in this zone of Devon still to find the little shut-away places. Lots of thatch, a cluster of cottages, a church on a hill. Perhaps 'cluster' is the wrong word: a cluster round the crossroads, yes; then a straggle up the combe—towards the Gabwells. But you mustn't go too far away from the crossroads: urban pressures increase rapidly here. But linger. Look at the rood screen, said to be one of Devon's earliest. Certainly very different from most. Look at the brass of John Symon, canon of Exeter and priest of Stoke. There he is in his vestments; and this brass is confidently declared to be the earliest in the county. "No great thing"? Somebody thought so—once.

From Newton Abbot to Torquay, along the A380, it's houses, houses practically all the way; almost totally enclosing the rural area just described. Only, as that road is approached, does Coffinswell preserve the rustic air so traditionally associated with Devon. Partly in this parish and partly in Haccombe-with-Combe, the enormous Iron Age camp, fort, or castle on Milber Down disputes Hembury's pre-eminence in sheer size, though lacking Hembury's sophisticated engineering. It stands as a metaphorical guardian of

Coffinswell's innocence. Court Barton, the old manor house, dating in its present form from the early sixteenth century and with fine granite mullions to its windows, is a mere newcomer. The tiny village itself is mostly cob and thatch and simplicity, but less and less able to maintain any real independence.

Kingskerswell is too large to be a village. In any case, it reaches out to Newton Abbot with one hand and to Torquay with the other. But Abbotskerswell, two miles west, inhabits a different world. Kerswell means 'cress well or spring' and this delightful place belonged to the Abbot of Horton (in Dorset) in 1086. Its church is old, its priory new, and the A381 is just far enough removed to leave the old nucleus undisturbed. Many a lovely Devon village has been ruined by a main road thrust through its heart. Abbotskerswell has escaped.

Marldon, on the other hand, is nearly engulfed. Its southern development takes it practically into Paignton; at the north end of the church, the Church House Inn and some cottages survive. Most visitors will pass through Marldon on their way to Compton Castle, the finest example of a fortified manor house in the whole of Devon. It is a surprising sight, situated where it is. There are quiet Devon lanes and then, suddenly, this gem of a place, built by Geoffrey Gilbert in the early fourteenth century, added to in the second half of the same century and extended in 1520. Gilberts lived there until 1800, Sir Humphrey—the most famous of them all—knowing it as home. And then, in the twentieth century, another Gilbert bought it back, restored it with loving care, and handed it over to the National Trust. So much has been written about Compton, its Gilbert deeds and Raleigh connections so romantically described, that competition is superfluous. The best advice is: see it for yourself and remember that Sir Humphrey's elder brother received from Queen Elizabeth a charter empowering him to "discover, search, find out and view such remote, heathen and barbarous lands not actually possessed of any Christian prince or people as to him shall seem good. . . ." From this rural Devon place great enterprises grew.

A few miles south-west stands Berry Pomeroy, taking its name partly from the earthworks (now deep in the woods north of the village) and partly from the Henry de la Pomeraye who held the manor in 1242. And Pomeroys and Seymours have held it ever since. The Pomeroys were Norman magnates with vast possessions. The Seymours played their chief role in history when one of them was Lord Protector in the reign of Edward VI. John Prince, who wrote *The Worthies of Devon*, was vicar of Berry Pomeroy and assures us that the Seymours spent £20,000 on the house in the seventeenth century, adding with one of those dry touches for which his book (not published until 1701) is noteworthy, "but never brought it to perfection". A comparatively late Seymour, a Speaker of the House of Commons, abandoned Berry for Maiden Bradley in Wiltshire, and when Prince made his comment the building was showing signs of neglect. It is a picturesque ruin now, not far removed in space, though much in time, from the earthworks deeper in the same woods.

The church that Seymours rebuilt and that John Prince served is far from decay. It has an impressive collection of monuments, Pomeroy and Seymour, a splendid screen and—not quite so apparent—an astonishing record of parsonical longevity. An incumbency of fifty years is quite common and two of its vicars spanned 111 years between them. It's not surprising, I suppose. They wouldn't be overburdened with work in this pretty little tightly-clustered place, which contrasts so strikingly with the castle remains, perched on a tree-surrounded rock high above the river. "All this glory", wrote Prince, "lieth in the dust, buried in its own ruins."

In the parish stands Longcombe Cross and near it a building known as Parliament House. The story commonly told of it is that William of Orange held his first parliament here. What actually happened was that on his way from Brixham to Berry Castle—where he was welcomed and entertained by Sir Edward Seymour—Dutch William paused here and received protestations of loyalty and promises of support from local dignitaries. The 'Glorious Revolution' could hardly fail to attract support in the West Country.

The best-known village in all Devon stands between the urban sprawls of Torquay and Paignton. Indeed, Cockington was one of the three ancient foundation parishes from which Torquay itself was formed. All sorts of nonsense has been talked about the place—inevitably, since about half a million people visit it every year. The fact that Chochintona ('Cocca's farm') is listed in

Domesday gave rise to the absurd belief that most of the buildings, and particularly the old forge and cottages, dated from at
least 1086. Torquay Corporation—as it used to be—looked after
the Court with great care and saw to it that the owners of the
village looked after that. The recent fuss about the date of the old
village buildings arose when the Torbay planning department
issued a report in connection with the proposal to make Cockington part of a conservation area. The report made a precise summary of historical facts that had been known but, in the nature
of things, little publicised: a manor here in 1086 with thirty-eight
inhabitants; acquired by the Carys in 1373; force-sold to the
Mallocks in 1654. Torquay Corporation bought the Court (which
Carys built in the sixteenth and seventeenth centuries and Mallocks part-classicized) for £50,000 in 1935. The Prudential Assurance Company bought the village and a lot of land round it in
1946 for . . . well, the price has never been disclosed but 'they say'
about £200,000.

What created the fuss was the 'revelation' that around 1800 all
the buildings except the church were swept away and new ones
built in their present position so that the view from the Court
should not be spoilt by the homes of the villagers.

There is nothing surprising about this. It was happening all
over England at that time. Cockington was one of the lucky
places: it got rebuilt. The houses that must not be seen from the
Court are now tourist meccas; and the Court itself is a publicly-
owned showpiece. "And thus the whirligig of time brings in his
revenges."

In 1934 a Lutyens-designed inn, 'The Drum', was built. Everything has to be 'in keeping' at Cockington. I'm sorry about the
pun, but the place is so perfect that it is very hard to take it seriously. It has become a sort of commercialised shrine and I don't
think I can do it justice except by quoting without comment the
words of a popular guide: "The pursuits of the village are agricultural, varied, in summer, by the business of ministering to the
needs of the visitors who flock hither in such numbers."

What some fear is that a good many Devon villages are heading for the same fate as Cockington, and that 'ministering to the
needs of the visitors who flock hither in such numbers' will become
the major occupation of Devonians. And that, in the long term,

will not be good for the villages, whether it proves remunerative for the Devonians or not.

South of A385 (Totnes to Paignton road) things improve. The Dart begins to assert itself and Tor Bay becomes a working sea again. The nearer you get to Brixham and Berry Head the more closely you are in touch with real life and creative occupations. There are not all that many villages left. They have mostly been slain by the kind of character assassination that falls under one of two headings: sub-urban (or commuter) villages, or 'holiday' villages which have been swallowed by the growth of resort towns. The irony of it is that these resort towns were themselves so short-a time ago mere villages. Yalberton (the name probably means 'the settlement on the stream lined with alders') just escapes engulfment by Paignton. It is still a hamlet rather than a village. Northwards, Collaton St Mary is chiefly of interest as the gateway to Blagdon Barton which, centuries ago, combined smallness with spaciousness. The house itself was a small medieval mansion but the manor was enormous, well over one thousand acres. The farm buildings that survive remind an observant traveller that this was a huge estate.

South again, and you are on the Dart; and entering, if you can find the way, what was once one of Devon's best villages. Getting to the outskirts of Stoke Gabriel is easy enough. Threading the maze of streets through the tofts and crofts is work for natives not foreigners. A friend of mine, a West Countryman who works and lives in London's literary world, has kept his home in Stoke Gabriel and spends all the time he can there. He has had the good sense to remain bi-lingual. 'R.P.' drops off his tongue effortlessly when he is in the metropolis. Back home in Devon he speaks either 'Oxford' (or what used to be called B.B.C.) English or his native tongue. At home, he makes a daily journey on foot to the delectable public house near the waterfront and is often appealed to for directions by car-borne foreigners. It is an interesting fact that he sometimes gets through to them better in Devonshire—accompanied by suitable gestures—than he does in his irreproachable 'middle class' English. There is a moment of shock when he switches tongues, but then they tune in and feel they are getting their money's worth.

Stoke Gabriel stands where a lovely creek opens off the Dart. The opposite banks are wooded and at Duncannon—good judges have claimed—are some of the river's loveliest reaches. The narrow, twisting streets of the little place, the exciting sense that the proximity of a great waterway stirs; the boats, the salmon, the church, Sandridge—where John Davis, the great Elizabethan explorer was born—these were the main ingredients of Stoke Gabriel's charm. There has been far too much 'development' recently and the bloom has gone.

On the west bank, too, there are some outstandingly lovely settlements. Ashprington stands on high ground between the Dart and Bow Creek and commands its isthmus with style and assurance. When Aescbeorht kept house here, long before the Normans came, he chose his spot with care. It is a very nicely grouped village culminating in church and pub, as it should. There is excellent twentieth-century woodwork in the church—the pulpit is especially good—to offset the results of a particularly aggressive 1880-ish onslaught. Down by the Dart the Sharpham estate, finely wooded, and gardens by Capability Brown, occupies nearly three miles of river frontage: worth a fortune today when everybody wants the fishing and the sailing and the holiday homes. Sharpham House was built out of prize money. Captain Philemon Pownall started the work in 1770, having received £65,000 from one capture alone. It was a dangerous version of 'the pools', though: he was killed in 1780, and Sharpham House was not finished for another forty years or so. It's not much to look at.

Much more fascinating is the riverside settlement 'at the oak enclosure' on the Wash river which runs into Bow Creek opposite Ashprington. There's a lovely winding road from the hill village, down through Bow to Tuckenhay, and then on to Cornworthy, and this road crosses both the Harbourne river and the Wash. These two waters have played a considerable part in Devon's industrial history. Yet how few of the thousands who come to the Dart for recreation either know or care about all this. At one time, the Harbourne powered at least seven mills including the famous Harbertonford Serge Mill. Harberton itself was the original settlement in the centre of a large and fertile parish. Totnes will rise in anger at the statement, but there is good evidence to show that it was once part of Harberton and was not split off until the tenth century. It is certain that Harbertonford did not become a separate parish until 1860. The separation of these two from the parent parish is of great historical interest. It is probable that Harberton parish once included all the land between the Dart and the Harbourne, the village itself being second in importance in this area only to Halwell which—incredible though it now seems—was once a *burh*. Then, sometime in the tenth century, Totnes also became a *burh*, minting its own coins in the reign of Edgar (959–75). Totnes's great leap forward did not, however, come until Norman times. It was the development of bigger ships and their employment in the all-important wine trade with the French possessions of the kings of England that made the great south coast estuaries important. Then places like Totnes, Dartmouth and Plymouth outstripped the inland settlements round which the Saxons had organized their life. Before the days of *cogs* and *nefs* and Bordeaux voyages, shelving beaches were the harbours, a few huts for gear constituted the fishing 'villages', and tracks led from these to the safety of the nucleated settlements well out of reach of marauders.

Harbertonford, on the other hand, attained its separate existence and its parochial status as the result of industrial progress. Its serge mill was famous, while at nearby Tuckenhay the paper mill (converted from cloth in 1830) was always busy. At the time of Harbertonford's breakaway, there was also a corn-mill and a sailcloth mill at Tuckenhay. A cider factory and quarries added to the wealth and work of the district, signallized most dramatically by the big quays at the mouth of the Harborne where ships of up to 160 tons could moor. It is not easy to believe in this Victorian energy when travelling through what is now such a rural area. The fourteenth- and fifteenth-century splendours of Harberton church and the lovely Church House Inn are the accustomed, the expected, attractions of a Devon village. The Victorian depredations within the church tell an all-too-familiar tale. How can the contrast be explained? One age of wealth—the fifteenth century —devoted its surplus to the creation of beauty. The Victorians, with the best intentions, swept so much away. Their own best creations—the little forges and factories dotted about a countryside which industry did very little to spoil (far less than tourism is doing)—are for the most part picturesque and interesting ruins.

Where they aimed at beauty, in their 'restorations', they usually left a mess behind.

All round Harberton are houses of great distinction: Domesday farms like East Leigh, West Leigh and Hazard (the name means 'Hereweald's bank'); Great Englebourne where not only can fragments of the early manor house be seen but the name preserves the memory of the earliest days of Saxon settlement: Englebourne, 'the boundary of the English'.

But this delectable district cannot fairly be claimed for the region we have called Torbay. Purists would argue that any settlement west of the Dart belongs to the South Hams; and Harberton and Halwell ('holy well' and very lovely) are several miles beyond the river. It is not so easy to be clear-cut, however, when following the windings of a long river, and it was the attractions—visual and historic—of the Harbourne that led this narrative into another region.

Nor is it easy to stop short on the east bank of the Dart, for the riverside settlements on both banks have common characteristics—economic, historic and recreational—as well as the topography that they so obviously share. Like many another natural feature of Devonshire, that great river, the Dart, must now be seen mainly in terms of its recreational use. There is boat building still, of course, and world-famous vessels are constructed in little yards. Timber-carrying ships go up-river to Totnes. Dartmouth is still an important harbour. But the commercial importance of the river derives from its use as a playground; a shift of emphasis that affects every village on its banks.

Boat-owners demand three basic facilities: parking space for cars, parking space for dinghies, launching and mooring spaces for larger boats. Given so magnificent a waterway as the Dart and so little else than agriculture to sustain the riverine population, the pressure to provide these facilities cannot be resisted. So many ancillary trades and occupations will flourish if the recreational use is expanded. When the motorway comes—so much of our thinking is dominated by that now—the facilities must be ready to reap the harvest. Hence, plans for marinas. Hence, the planning for extra deep-water moorings between Dittisham and Stoke Gabriel. Hence, the enormous changes that will occur in the next few years. The River Dart Navigation Commissioners control the

river from the Dittisham/Greenway Quay in the south to Totnes
Weir in the north. They are seeking more car-parking facilities
and access to the river, particularly in the Dittisham and Greenway area. Totnes Rural Council has accepted the need for 'adequate
parking and access' in their territory. Messrs Philip and Son, boat
builders of Kingswear, have plans for greatly increased activities
lower down the river. Within ten years, it is estimated, there may
be moorings for five hundred boats *above* Dittisham. Anything
written now about an area so palpably on the brink of vast changes
must be very tentative.

Dittisham—'Dodda's ham'—is where they grow the plums. It is
also, of course where they sail the boats. It has a lovely slate-built
church—a feature of villages in this area—and though there is not
a lot left of the church that stood here in 1333, the fifteenth
century did its customary magnificent job. Its 'wineglass' pulpit
is superb. Of the Pugin windows, Professor Pevsner says coldly
that they are "rather like the glass one sees in Victorian board-
ing-houses". But nobody comes here to look at indifferent stained
glass; they come for the river. There is a ferry to Greenway on the
other side, and in the river, lower down, is the Anchor Stone, on
which Sir Walter Raleigh is said to have smoked one of those innumerable 'first pipes'. Though why he should have chosen to sit
or stand there for the purpose must surely baffle anybody who
chooses to take the nonsense seriously. He had undoubted connections with Greenway House, for his three famous Gilbert half-
brothers were born there. Sir John Gilbert, the eldest of them,
became Lord Sheriff and Vice-Admiral of Devon, sharing with
George Cary of Cockington the task of guarding Drake's Spanish
prisoners taken when the *Rosario* was captured. He used them to
terrace his Greenway gardens: an arrangement that Cary dis-
approved of. Greenway—the house is not the original one—is
the home of Dame Agatha Christie, of *Mousetrap* fame.

The main reason for having a ferry here is to provide a link
with Galmpton and Churston Ferrers. Galmpton stands at the
head of its own creek and is in Churston Ferrers' parish, while
Churston occupies a spacious site that almost fills the gap between Tor Bay and the Dart Estuary. Both, I think, are as unmistakably Torbay villages as Halwell and Harberton belong to the
South Hams. Indeed, close comparison between each pair will teach

the traveller much about these two very different regions and will discourage him from making easy generalizations about Devonshire. Both the Torbay villages are in Domesday and each had a strategic significance which the Saxons were quick to grasp.

Yet I cannot be very hopeful about the lovely, lower banks of the Dart. The hand of the developer will lie heavy on them yet, I fear; though the river from Dartmouth to Totnes must provide some of the finest sights in the whole of ·Britain. And both Dartmouth and Totnes, and their associated villages, have been—in Leland's phrase—fine things.

North of the Totnes-Buckfastleigh road, and enclosed by the A38 to the west and the A381 to the east, the villages are safer. Westwards, the land rises and the settlements there are more appropriately considered in the Dartmoor chapter. Eastwards, they have a Torbay flavour, yet generally escape the pressures that bear so heavily on the villages nearer to the resort belt.

Just north of the A384 and enclosed by a huge bend of the Dart is that varied complex of educational, rural-industrial and cultural activities and experiments known to the whole world as Dartington Hall. "An essay in the reconstruction of rural life", the whole great enterprise has been called. Not only Devon, but all England, owes much to the vision of those pioneers, the Elmhirsts. And if some ventures had a touch of preciousness and some were viable only when backed by a fortune selflessly spent, much that is solid and more that is imaginative has been created. Farms, forestry, drama, music, builders, contractors (Staverton), sawmills, educational experiment, glass, the Dartington Amenity Research Trust . . . the list seems endless. *Trust* indeed! Faith: faith that rural life could be revitalized in an increasingly urban environment. Noble. Justified? Who can say—yet? Too few Dartingtons. Too much monopoly capitalism. Too many people pressing on the land and devouring its resources.

Apart from the Dartington enterprise there, Staverton has been famous for its cider almost as long as apples have been pressed. Its limekilns are now on the official list of 'industrial archaeology' in the county. Its bridge is one of Devon's best medieval relics. It has a much-praised church too.

North and east of Staverton a countryside opens up that is

redolent of the county's very founding. Broadhempston ('the great farm belonging to *Haeme*') stands pleasantly as ever it did and is of particular interest to historians as being one of the very few parishes to possess pre-Reformation churchwardens' accounts. A splendid pub and a fine church, neighboured by Littlehempston (oh fortunate *Haeme*!), what a spot to choose as an exploration centre.

And a few miles east stands Ipplepen. It isn't, it must be confessed, all that much to look at. There has been too much bad building recently for its character to survive; but the church is good, especially the nave windows and the pulpit. It is the name that is so important: Ipplepen—'Ippela's hill'; and Ippela (or Hyple) was a Celtic name. And only a mile or so north-west is Denbury: 'the fort of the men of Devon'—*Defnas burh*. You could not find clearer proof that Saxon and Celt existed side by side; that Saxon settlement did not entail Celtic extermination. Denbury was established as a Saxon settlers' stronghold *west* of Ipplepen, yet Ippela the Celt was left in peaceful possession of his hill. There was plenty of room. The great fort from which Denbury took its name —though the fort was there before the Saxons arrived and occupied it and named it—stands on a hill overlooking the village. The hill is volcanic; fittingly so, I always think. Denbury is one of the failed boroughs of Devon. It got a market in 1286, having then for many years belonged to Tavistock Abbey, and sometime in the fourteenth century it became officially a 'town'. But the venture did not succeed. Just as well, perhaps. It might have lost its nice Tudor and Jacobean buildings in the main street. The massive chimney breasts backing onto the road are found in a few Devon villages but are really much more characteristic of Somerset.

Nearby Torbryan should not be missed by anybody who loves pubs and churches—and there is not much point in exploring villages if you lack the passion for both. The Church House Inn *was* the church house. It dates back to about 1500: to about the time, in fact, that Sir William Petre was born at Tornetown, not far away. The builders of the church house little knew what havoc that newborn baby was destined to wreak on monastic lands. As a Secretary of State in four reigns he was well placed to pull out many a plum and found from ecclesiastical spoils a landed dynasty. Torbryan church is held by some good judges to be "the most uniformly attractive village church in Devon". A list of its attractions would be long and tedious. The only thing to do is to see it for yourself; and try to get a sight of the bells. They are the originals, cast in Exeter in the reign of Henry VI.

Prolonged argument would not resolve the problem of whether the now narrowing corridor between the A38 and the A380 more properly belongs to the Torbay region or to Dartmoor and its skirts. I indicate my own preference in saying that I like to see it as part of that broad wedge of exciting country through which one travels south-westward-bound from Exeter: heading for Moreton-hampstead along that infuriating yet charming cart track called B3212, with side roads beckoning at every turn, and the enchantment of Dartmoor ahead.

It is among the approaches to Dartmoor that I shall describe such villages as Shillingford and Dunchideock, Ide and Chudleigh. They do not belong to the Torbay sub-region.

5

The South Hams

ALTHOUGH the name 'South Hams' is of great antiquity, even now a surprisingly large number of people cannot identify the area to which it refers. This is true not only of visitors to the county—even of some who take holidays in the South Hams!—but of Devonians themselves. For many a year past it could be argued that such ignorance was not wholly bad. The area, was, to a large extent, protected by not being known. Its visitors were discriminating and comparatively few, and its distinctive qualities seemed safe. Pressure built up, however, and the formation of the South Hams Society in 1961 was a much needed response to threats that were then becoming apparent, particularly the felling of fine timber and the widespread construction of ugly buildings. The work of the society has been greatly admired and has done much to remove ignorance about the South Hams. The imaginative attitude of the Devon County Council planning department and committee has also had a special relevance to this superb area. Devon County Council, it may be noted, struggles hard to be on the side of the angels—it was the first authority, for example, to appoint a conservation officer—and, however easy it may be to find fault with details of its work, it would be very hard for any reasonable critic to fault its overall approach, having regard to the special problems of a county, so beautiful, so desired and so poor.

If there has been ignorance about the very existence of a distinctive area called the South Hams this has been matched by vigorous debate over its precise boundaries. I do not think that we need be in any great doubt. The eastern border of the South Hams is the

Dart from Totnes to the sea. The western boundary is the Plym. The northern boundary is the A385 from Totnes to Avonwick; and from Avonwick to its junction with the A38, which then bounds the area in as far as the head of the Plym estuary. Its southern boundary is the sea, some of the finest headlands and bays in the whole of Britain distinguishing this fine South Hams coastline.

Because it was convenient to treat the two banks of the lower Dart as an entity, the closing pages of the last chapter were concerned with settlements that are technically within the South Hams; and the attractions of the Harbourne valley led deep into South Hams territory. It is high time, then, to attempt a characterization of the setting as a whole and to describe the strong South Hams individuality to which its villages make their own distinctive contribution.

'The pastures south of Dartmoor' are enclosed on three sides by the sea: the high land to the north shelters them from the worst weather; the great estuaries of the south coast bite deep into the land. All those factors shape the life of this region, resulting as they do in a temperate climate and in long north-south valleys that present formidable barriers to communication. It was the high wilderness of Dartmoor in the north and the Dart valley in the east that for so long shut the South Hams off from the main stream of county life and tourist traffic.

Again, the geology is distinctive. Some of the oldest rocks in the county have weathered into the striking shapes and varied hues that mark the coast between Start Point and Bolt Tail. Wide bands of Devonian sandstones, limestones and slates rise in regular steps between the sea and the moor, deeply cut across their grain by four big rivers, all of which are born on Dartmoor. The soil, though varying considerably, is well drained and warm in the slate and limestone belts. The frequency of valleys gives great diversity to this rolling countryside: rich meadows in the valley bottoms, very fair pasture higher up and arable on the rounded tops. There is not a lot of woodland—the hills, indeed, are almost treeless—but there is fine hedgerow timber and a most picturesque network of hedge-topped high banks surrounding and dividing the small-to-medium mixed farms.

The emphasis is on dairying and here, indeed, was the traditional home of that remarkable triple-purpose breed, the South-Devon, famous for milk, butterfat and beef. Friesians outnumber it now, in the South Hams as elsewhere.

The villages, as befits a land that the Saxons colonized, are nucleated. Slate is a much-used building material; a local slate that weathers kindly and is frequently a barely observed background for the lush growth of plant and creeper—native or exotic—that the warm wetness of the climate encourages in such abundance.

A basic exploration plan for the South Hams villages could be constructed on the region's most remarkable topographical feature: its dissection by the estuaries and their rivers. Working from west to east, there would then be four north-south strips divided by the Yealm, the Erme and the Avon. Add to this the many-armed salt-water opening of Salcombe Harbour, extending inland as far as Kingsbridge, and the area would split into five vertical strips.

There is another possibility. There are two nodal points in the South Hams: Kingsbridge (the 'capital') and Modbury. Either of these offers what in this dissected land pass for good communications and can be used as an exploration centre. (Kingsbridge is, of course, a town not a village.) In her excellent book *The South Hams* Margaret Willy suggested Malborough as a third possibility. It is certainly the ideal centre from which to explore the wonderful Bolt Head district.

However, since the Harbourne valley has already been mentioned and the South Hams district has been opened up as far south as Halwell, it is logical to return now to that little place. Two earthworks—Halwell Camp itself and Stanborough—both now greatly damaged by roads, testify to a life more ancient than the Saxon settlement; and west of Stanborough a section of ridgeway goes back even further in time. It is believed that Stanborough kept watch for possible landings on the beaches of Start Bay and that it and Halwell may have been links in a signalling chain, as well as strong points. All the way from Halwell to Kingsbridge that ancient ridgeway at times merges with, at times diverges from, the A381. The road lifts sharply after Halwell and keeps up all the way until, in the parish of Buckland-tout-Saints it dips down to Kingsbridge.

Interesting villages lie east and west of this road. Blackawton—

(left) A fine bench-end at Holbeton. *(right)* Bridford's lovely pulpit

la Memoire de Louis
MBROISE QUANTI
HEUZEN du la *4e*
ég du Corps *Imper*
l d'Artillerie de
arine Agé de 53 Ans
écédé le 29 d'Avril
1810.

(above) Aveton Gifford
church

(left) A French soldier's
tombstone in the porch
Moretonhampstead churc

The famous Fulford tomb in Dunsford church

Old granite cottages at
Throwleigh

there is a lot of argument about the meaning of the name—was
the central settlement in a very large parish before Strete was
taken out in the late nineteenth century. 'Black', it has been suggested, derives from the colour of the slate used in many of the
buildings, which deepens dramatically in hue when it is wet;
'awton' could mean 'Alfa's farm', but may derive from 'Avon',
meaning river. The latter guess is reinforced by the South Hams
name Aveton Gifford, which is pronounced 'Awton Jifford'. A
tributary of the Gara rises near Blackawton and could well have
been simply 'the Avon'. It is a large well-planned village standing
at a valley head, and in the mid-nineteenth century it was of some
importance as the centre of a thriving agricultural district, supplying a wide range of goods and services to the scattered farms and
hamlets as well as to its own inhabitants. Modern transport and
the reduced manpower of modern agriculture have ended such a
function for villages such as Blackawton. There are many relics of
bygone importance: the memorials, font and rood screen in the
church—the screen bears the initials of Henry VIII and Catherine
of Aragon, a stroke of dramatic irony—the very considerable farmhouses, some retaining traces of manorial splendour; and Fuge,
first recorded in 1269, its name telling us that it was the 'cattle
farm' of the royal manor that Blackawton once was.

Harold Bate, the inventor, has brought new fame to Blackawton. His chicken-manure-fuelled car was not a commercial success—though it worked well enough. His latest device, a self-pro-
pelled bike using vibrations from bumps in the road to pick up speed,
is just at the development stage as these words are written.

From Blackawton a maze of lanes, deep sunken and their banks
gay with the wild flowers which are a chief glory of the South
Hams, leads—if that is the right verb—through hamlets like
Millcombe and East Allington back to the main Kingsbridge road.
Cross it, and come to Loddiswell—recorded in Domesday and the
site of Lodd's spring. The name is more poetical than the place
but I do not share in the general disparagement of Loddiswell. It
seems to have survived its modern extensions pretty well and the
old 'square' village is evident. It makes a good base from which to
explore the Avon, the valley of which has a dramatic beauty that
heightens with every northbound mile. Then, too, there is the intriguing case of Blackdown Camp (or Loddiswell Rings, to give its

G

alternative name), which was quite clearly a twelfth-century castle, though nobody knows who built or owned it. Near it, a great ridgeway leads from Dartmoor to the sea. The Avon, which flows through wooded country east of Loddiswell and for several miles north of that village, like many another Devon name is not pronounced as it is spelt. It is called the 'Awn' and this would distinguish it very neatly from all the other Avons, if only 'foreigners' knew how to pronounce it.

Aveton Gifford is 'the farm by the river Avon' and it was held by Walter Giffard in 1242. It is a pretty place and had one of the oldest churches in Devon until it was almost completely destroyed by a German bomb in 1943. These little places—Loddiswell is another—had to supply an astonishing number of salmon to Judhel of Totnes, who, after the Conquest, held nearly forty thousand acres of the South Hams. Loddiswell paid thirty salmon a year and so did Cornworthy.

But Aveton Gifford should be remembered chiefly for Robert Macey, born here in 1790. He became a celebrated architect and built many famous London buildings, including the 'Adelphi' and the 'Haymarket'. His story is the more remarkable in that he was the son of a mason. It was not easy for him to make his way as he did.

The settlements at the mouth of the Avon are disappointing. The most interesting thing about Bigbury is its name, derived from Borough Island. The island once had a chapel on its summit, but there is nothing left of that now. Bigbury-on-Sea is pure holiday land and 'New' Thurlestone has nothing much to show. 'Old' Thurlestone, however, is a delight. A fine church—local slate—and some very good cottages. The name is derived from the wave-pierced (or 'thirled') rock off shore, a natural feature important enough to be mentioned in a charter of 845. In any case, striking or otherwise in themselves, these coastal villages know how to make visitors welcome and offer excellent opportunities for exploring a fascinating seaside.

West of the Avon, the Erme is flanked near its mouth by Kingston and Holbeton. Kingston is an attractive little place, nicely grouped, with many good houses and an earlier church than is common. Wonwell Court, a mile or so away, has been much praised for its handsome hooded porch. Its name is very curious.

It was the dwelling of Wunbeald or Wunstan, but it was his pet-name that was enshrined. He seems to have been nicknamed Wunna and it stuck.

On the other side of the river, Holbeton ('the farm in the hollow land') is so remarkable that it might well be the perfect pattern of a South Hams village. There are not many monuments in the whole of Devon to equal the Hele tomb with its twenty-two kneeling figures arranged in four tiers. They represent four genera-tions and are so placed as to focus attention on the central reclin-ing figure, Sir Richard himself. He receives their devotion com-placently. Unusual, too, is the excellent modern woodwork: screens, benches and stalls. The whole of the interior of All Saints is lavish but in perfect taste. Indeed, Holbeton and its surroundings radiate a serenity that defies the pressures of the present. The banks of the Erme sustain a noteworthy cluster of country houses, the most notable—in size and antiquity, if not architecturally—being Flete (the navigable point of the river: *fleot*) a Saxon estate.

Further up-river, and on its banks, is Ermington, founded very early in the Saxon settlement, listed as a royal manor in Domes-day, and the 'capital' of a hundred. It is famous, of course, for its twisted spire, but the age of that same spire—all of it belongs to the late thirteenth century—is at least as remark-able as it shape. The village is so neatly planned, too: a spacious square surrounded by houses and shops; a pleasant pub; the church on a slope above the square. Very satisfactory indeed, and very hard to spoil. The parish abounds with ancient houses; several are in Domesday, but the most fascinating of all is Pen-quit which missed Domesday, though its Celtic name ('end of the wood') attests occupation of the site before the Saxons came and, more importantly, continued British occupation after they settled the district. Every other place-name for miles around is unmis-takably Anglo-Saxon, but the inhabitants of Penquit were left in peace; and left the name behind them.

If Modbury were left out of this book there would be justifiable complaints. Yet to include it in a book on villages is to risk hurt-ing its civic pride. However, as it qualifies on population—it falls well short of 1,500 inhabitants—and is an altogether delightful place, the ancient *burh* will perhaps recognize that no slight is intended. It was a borough by 1238 with a weekly market and

two fairs. Until near the end of the nineteenth century St George's
Fair was the great annual event in the South Hams. Nine days of
merrymaking and ten inns open from morning till night. What
more could anyone ask? Dancing in the streets; stalls flaring with
naphtha and glittering with gew-gaws; even private houses dis-
playing the bush that proclaimed 'here is good ale to be had'.
The celebrated 'white ale' of Kingsbridge, for which the South
Hams was once so famous, was said to be incomparable when
'tuned' with a full glass of old Jamaica rum, preferably that on
which no duty had been paid. Many a gallon flowed at St George's
Fair. It's a quiet occasion now: one day only and mostly a cattle
sale—but still proclaimed on St George's Eve. Though there is
very little white ale or 'tuning' in these less vigorous days.

The hillside to which Modbury clings provides a dramatic setting for an attractive collection of buildings, many of which belong
to the late eighteenth and early nineteenth centuries when its
population was growing. They descend the street in careful order,
their doorways, bays and slated fronts making a most pleasing
composition. The Exeter Inn and the 'White Hart', indeed, the
whole of Church Street, give delight. St George's, at the west end,
is described as 'quite remarkable' and its spire—set very firmly
on top of a low tower—is visible for many a mile around. The
experts are not in agreement about the date of the spire, some
saying that it is the original medieval construction, others believing that it is an exact copy, built after lightning struck in 1621.
But all agree on the unusual effect. Whatever the truth, the church
presents a fine sight; a most pleasing combination of spaciousness
and quaintness.

Not far from Modbury is the battlefield where, in 1643, a Parliamentary force broke the Royalists, the honours of the day traditionally belonging to the Devonshire clubmen whose valour and
zeal overwhelmed their better-equipped enemies. Inevitably, the
story goes that the Parliamentary troops signalized their contempt
for King and episcopacy by stabling their horses in Modbury church
after the battle. A lot of Devon churches seem to have suffered
this sacrilege!

Making use of Modbury's focal situation, the South Hams explorer can travel west, crossing the Erme and then leaving the
main road as soon as possible to head for those twin delights—

Newton Ferrers and Noss Mayo. Here, in the extreme south-western borders of the region, lie what many regard as the finest villages of them all. Newton was given to Henry de Ferrières as part of his share of the loot after the Conquest. The map of Devon is littered with 'Ferrers', showing how well he did out of the business. Noss belonged to Matthew, son of John, a much smaller man than Henry de Ferrières, but nevertheless a considerable land-owner in this remote corner. This particular little Noss (*ness* or 'promontory') of his must surely have been among his most favoured possessions.

Newton tumbles very prettily down to the waterfront, to which feature its little main street, garden paths and alleyways all hurry. There is a delightful walk up the river towards Bridgend—all painted boats on this side and trees on the other and waterside cottages. At Bridgend—where, before there was a bridge, the cross-ing was made on stepping stones—there's an old mill and Post Office Farm, and more concentrated nostalgia than is common even in Devon—a county that tends to dream of a golden age that never existed; at least, not in the form of which the dreamers talk. It is true, of course, that the district was, within living memory, part of a great estate and that in the Edwardian era feudal magnifi-cence glittered at Membland Hall—now a mere shell and a hand-ful of gardeners' cottages and lodges. True, too, that at both New-ton and Noss new buildings have appeared: commuters to Ply-mouth, retired people, week-end sailors, all find the twin villages attractive and convenient. Yet, I wonder—did the tight hold of banking and landowning wealth and the fondly-recalled visits of crowned or at least coronetted heads do all that much? Or, put it at its lowest, has recent popularity and building been so very much worse?

Noss Mayo has a new church and an old one. It is in the ancient parish of Revelstoke and the old church, early fourteenth-century, was built far out of the village, standing in an exposed position near Stoke Point. A couple of miles was nothing for people to walk in those days and the church made an excellent landmark for sailors on this perilous coast. In softer times—1882, to be exact—the new St Peter's was built in Noss itself and the old church decayed into a most beautiful ruin. Holy Cross in Newton looks just slightly contemptuously at the parvenu across the water.

The mazy creeks up-river from the twin villages lead eventually to Brixton and Yealmpton. Brixton is tiny, but it is the centre of one of the most remarkable clusters of Domesday buildings to be found in the whole of Devon. Brixton itself was there, of course, in 1086, but so were Chittleburn and Halwell, Hareston, Sherford and Spriddlestone. In the village are some lovely cottages and, very near the church, a most beautiful medieval house. It may have been the church house or even the parsonage at one time. But most people will remember Brixton for its elms. They were planted in 1667 by Edward Fortesque of Spriddlestone, to be felled 'when ready' for the relief of the poor in the parish. When is an elm ready? When it has Dutch elm disease?

Whereas Brixton stands between two waters, Yealmpton ('Yampton' in the Devon tongue) is down by the river, its centre a little removed from the bridge and the mill. Old Tristram Risdon, writing in the seventeenth century, was moved to an eloquent outburst: Yealmpton, he said, was "the chief begotten of the river Yealm where, according to tradition, the Saxon King Ethelwold had his palace". A more certain though less dignified connection is with Old Mother Hubbard. She was housekeeper at Kitley in 1805 and inspired Sarah Martin, sister-in-law of the squire, to produce the well-known rhymes. Puslinch, not far away, also has literary associations. It belonged to the Yonge family in Victorian times and Charlotte M. Yonge, who wrote *The Heir of Redclyffe* and many another tear-jerker, spent her holidays there.

Yealmpton church was rebuilt by Butterfield in 1850 and Sir John Betjeman has called it "the most amazing Victorian church in Devon". It depends, I suppose, on what he means by 'amazing'. Anyway, it is worth a visit. And for those whose taste inclines them to curiosities of another kind, the whole district abounds in ghost stories and witch lore. Peter Perrin's ghost brought about the destruction of Membland Hall. He specialized in very skilful driving of a phantom carriage-and-pair, while both Newton and Noss were well-known for their witches. I believe they all disappeared when the estate broke up.

Back east, on and near the Salcombe inlet, the superb countryside is dominated by the high plateau on which Malborough stands—and has stood since the day when that fine hill belonged to Maerla, and took its name from him. We do not know much about him but that his name is enshrined in this delightful village. We *do* know that this part of the South Hams was settled in early Saxon times. The innumerable creeks and inlets of Salcombe and Kingsbridge opened easy routes for ship-borne, land hungry farmers. Here, as round Brixton, is another cluster of Domesday manors; and though—like most fishing villages—it had to await more peaceful days, Hope was established early in the thirteenth century. Malborough's famous broach spire—rising straight out of its low west tower—dominates the scene. It is a lovely church with plenty of light and space. They used Beer stone here to great advantage in the fifteenth-century arcades. Then, in 1870, during a so-called restoration, the huge rood screen was demolished. It really is not possible to understand how such an act of vandalism could have been perpetrated.

Nothing has happened, however, to spoil Malborough itself. It is for many the crown of the South Hams; and the gateway to the 'Bolt', that incomparable cliff stretch between Head and Tail, with Hope nestling in the shelter of the latter.

There are two Hopes—Outer Hope and Inner Hope. You must not be disappointed by Outer. It is all new and quite uninteresting. Inner Hope is superb. It gets overcrowded in the summer, of course. All our coastal villages do, which is why true enthusiasts prefer the less obvious charms of such moorland settlements as have not yet got themselves well known.

No connoisseur of the South Hams could fail to add to his list of favourite villages the lovely settlement of Ringmore. The place-name experts say that it means a 'tract of land cleared of wood and undergrowth'. If so, one can only agree that the job was thoroughly done. Situated at the apex of an inverted triangle the base of which is formed by Kingston and Bigbury, it really is a gem. Cottages built mostly of stone; tall, crooked chimneys; abundant thatch—it seems to grow out of the landscape. It's utterly harmonious with its surroundings; and what a name for a pub—the 'Journey's End'! The claim that part of that inn dates back to 1300 may be true or false for all I know. It doesn't matter. Pub and church are as near contemporary as makes no difference. Bodily and spiritual food. Oh, blessed Ringmore!

East of the great octopus-like tentacles of Salcombe-Kings-

bridge, set amidst coastal scenery that rivals even 'The Bolt',
Chivelstone, East Prawle, South Allington and Stokenham cry out
for attention. And, hard by Stokenham, one of Devon's more
fantastic features astonishes the traveller. A raised beach divides
Slapton Ley from the open waters of Start Bay. The whole area
behind the Ley—though, strictly, we should speak of 'the Leys',
since the fresh-water lake divides into Slapton Ley and Lower
Ley—was taken over by the American Army in 1943-4 and battle
exercises were practised throughout the once-peaceful countryside. The beach itself and the waters of the Ley were of particular
value in preparing amphibious forces for the Normandy landings
of June 1944. An obelisk on the beach now memorializes this fading historical event, which seemed—and, no doubt, was—a good
idea at the time. It is increasingly difficult for us, even for those
who were alive and involved, to accept the necessity then invoked
for even a temporary evacuation of this lovely land. People,
animals, homes—all sacrificed to war. However, some things go
onwards the same, 'though dynasties pass'; and life has now
returned.

Slapton itself is the key settlement in the area. Its most remarkable feature is the remains of Sir Guy de Brien's collegiate chantry. He was lord of the manor here in the reign of Edward III and
standard-bearer to that formidable monarch. In 1373 he founded
his chantry and left posterity to wonder at it. It was at about the
same time that the low west tower of St James's church was crowned
with a spire, but the village itself long pre-dates both. Its name
means 'the tun (farm or settlement) by the slippery place', and
Slapton lies low where the contours slide swiftly to the waters.
There is a lot of thatch and thick-walled, huddled stone cottages,
many of which have those deep Devon porches, so cool on a summer's day and so sheltering in winter.

A little to the north, Strete was cut out of Blackawton in the
late nineteenth century, though its church considerably antedates
its separate eccleslastical and parochial identity. It is not very old,
not very remarkable, but very pleasant indeed; not requiring—
though receiving—reflected glory from Stoke Fleming and Blackpool.

The enchanting little cove called Blackpool was once the scene
of deeds so great as to merit a *Te Deum* in Westminster Abbey.

In the reign of Henry IV a Breton force landed here with the intention of plundering Dartmouth in retaliation for injuries inflicted upon France by the seamen of that town. They were overwhelmed by the local levies, partly because, in the hope of achieving surprise, the cavalry pressed on ahead of their cross-bowmen. They were mown down by Devon archers—a sort of rehearsal for Agincourt. A contemporary French chronicler recorded sadly that "the crows have pecked the eagles".

Stoke Fleming perches high on a hilltop above Blackpool. It must be one of the most delightful villages in all the South Hams. Though the church was ruthlessly restored in 1871 there is plenty left to see, especially the tower arch effigy of Elizabeth Mohun. Another fine memorial is the huge brass to John Corp and his grand-daughter—"she of the dainty form and flying veil". This is reckoned by experts to be one of the best brasses in Devon. But, then, there is a lot about Stoke Fleming that demands superlatives. Those narrow streets, and the path along the cliffs, and old Elias Newcomen's memorial: "in knowledge old, in zeal of life most grave". Elias died just before Shakespeare did, yet his great-grandson was that Thomas Newcomen who invented the steam engine. So brief a span it seems; but what different worlds the two men inhabited.

Perhaps that is the final impression that these South Hams villages make on the traveller—they impose an historical perspective, compounded of the smiling countryside out of which they spring and their own antiquity. Here, our Saxon forefathers made some of their earliest settlements. Motor cars and visitors, tractors and milk tankers, ice-cream and frozen foods cannot obliterate the pervading sense of their life and work.

6

Dartmoor and the Tamar Valley

WIND your way through St Thomas—once a village, but now wholly absorbed by the fair city of Exeter—and take the A30 for a mile or so. At the bottom of the hill, follow the B3212 instead of bearing right for Okehampton. As you climb steeply towards Longdown you cannot fail to be aware that you are entering an enchanted land. The road itself can be infuriating. It is twisty and up-and-down: wholly unsuited to the volume of traffic that it now must carry. There are nasty bits of between-the-wars 'development' here and there. But you are heading for Moreton-hampstead and the 'Warren House' and Postbridge and Two Bridges and. . . ! You are heading, in short, for Dartmoor, one of England's few surviving wildernesses, under whose stern heights and shaggy flanks nestle some of the loveliest and most historic villages in the county of Devon. And every turning off this wonderful road that bisects 'The Forest' will lead to ancient settlements, beauty, quaintness, farms that were here before the Saxons came, old industrial sites, 'tin churches', grim granite pounds.

But don't rush. Cover first the crescent-shaped territory between the westward-running A30 and the A38, so busily making its way south. Here, in the approaches to Dartmoor, are sequestered, unspoilt places where time seems to stand still because change has as yet done so little to spoil them. At the top of Duns-ford Hill a road leads off to Ide—or you may prefer to take the next turning and go through the water-splash. Ide (pronounced 'Ede') takes its name from St Ida, its patron saint. It is a delightful rural spot, straggling uphill along its one main street which begins soon after the ancient bridge spans the river Alphin. There is argument about the river's name, some authorities believing that both stream and village were once called Ide. Whatever the truth, the place is a vivid example of the way in which a crossing place created a community.

Shillingford (or Shillingford St George, to give it full honours) and Dunchideock are rival villages having interesting names, Dunchideock being the older of the two and victor in the struggle fought out many years ago. 'Shilling' has nothing to do with currency: the traveller did *not* have to pay a shilling to cross the ford. (The story is still told, despite its manifest absurdity.) Sciella was a long-forgotten Anglo-Saxon who once owned the settlement.

Dunchideock beats it hollow in antiquity. The name is pure Celtic, meaning 'the wooded camp or fort'. The reference is undoubtedly to the earthworks at Cotley, about a mile and a half north-west of the village. The lovely little church of St Michael is remarkable for the beauty and interest of its furnishings, the rood screen being perhaps its most noteworthy feature. Hannah More wrote General Stringer Lawrence's epitaph in the church. He became known as 'the father of the Indian Army' for he commanded the East India Company's troops in the mid-eighteenth century. Lawrence left his enormous fortune to Sir Robert Palk, of Haldon House, who erected the Haldon Belvedere in his benefactor's memory. But it is the place itself that enchants, lying as it does in the skirts of Haldon and marked as it is by a living spirit.

No Devonian can hear the name 'Dunchideock' without thinking of the 'treacle mines'. It's an old joke; and the better for its antiquity. It has been revived to good effect by the present owner of Dunchideock House, who, full of good humour and ingenuity, dreams up imaginative schemes to keep the little church well cared for. Every two years a fête is held in the grounds of his beautiful house. This is a kind of entertainment not usually high on my list of desirable activities, but Dunchideock is different. Its fête is as lively and original as its annual harvest-home supper: nothing self-conscious or forced about either. The house itself presents a good-looking early Georgian exterior which conceals much older features. It is redolent of the village in its charm and style.

The great victory that Dunchideock scored over Shillingford is remembered without rancour. A Dunchideock man once obtained a

Parliamentary decree ordering that Shillingford should build a gallery in its church to accommodate visitors from Dunchideock. The order, though never enforced, is still on the statutes! Even Shillingford's celebrated Huddesfield-Courtenay brass cannot quite efface that memory.

To the south, up-over-and-under Haldon, lies Chudleigh. It lies on a hill but in a hollow and it may well be that 'Chud' derives from the Old English word meaning 'bag'. No disrespect is intended in mentioning this. Topographically, the Saxon nickname fits well. In any case, one of Devon's most famous products—chudleighs and cream—is a noteworthy testimonial to the honour of its name. It is even now very near the population limit to warrant inclusion in this book, but it's such a delightful place that exclusion would be near sacrilege. It owed its rise to its key position on the Exeter-Plymouth road and used to boast a market and three fairs. Like many another old Devon 'town' it suffered serious decline in the nineteenth century and this followed—as again was common—disastrous eighteenth-century fires. Such conflagrations were usually ascribed to the wickedness of the inhabitants but in fact were caused by cob and thatch construction and inadequate water for fire-fighting.

What can be said of Chudleigh in a small space? 'Go and see for yourself,' is really the only advice. St Martin's has a most unusual tower and an interior that epitomizes seven hundred years of Devon's history. Next to the church is the lovely old grammar school founded in 1668; and hardly a street or turning fails to offer some evidence of Chudleigh's past importance.

At the time of writing there is what has been aptly called 'a storm in a beer mug' in Chudleigh. Professor Pevsner described the 'Clifford Arms' as "a modest early nineteenth-century hotel" (*The Buildings of England: South Devon*) and selected it for brief mention. If that dating is right—and the Professor's authority is not to be questioned lightly—then the beer mug storm is the more interesting. The present landlord and licensee intends not only to spend a great deal of money on improvements but also to change the name to the 'Old Coaching House'. He believes that the hotel bore that name to begin with. He could well be right, since the date of the building and Chudleigh's importance as a staging post would support him. However, Lord Clifford of Chudleigh, whose family has lived at nearby Ugbrooke for over three hundred years, is anxious that the name should not be changed. The Chudleigh Parish Council feels the same, regretting the loss of a visible connection between Chudleigh and the Cliffords. The new owner, faced with what he regarded as interference, has sturdily proclaimed his intention of going ahead, so the 'Clifford Arms' may well be the 'Old Coaching House' by the time this book is in print. The incident provides yet another illustration of the interest always aroused, and of the excitement often stirred, when an inn's name is changed.

Ugbrooke is of great interest, having been the seat of Thomas Clifford of 'Cabal' fame. He was Lord Treasurer to Charles II and was created Lord Clifford of Chudleigh by that monarch. He built the first house here (the present one is the result of a rebuilding in 1760) and included a chapel which the then Bishop of Exeter consecrated, not knowing that Clifford was to become an open Roman Catholic!

The park at Ugbrooke ('Ucga's Brook': it sounds better like that) is very beautiful. A large expanse of some six hundred acres, an upper and lower lake and hills all around; one of which is known as 'Dryden's Seat', for that great poet was a frequent visitor here in the days of Thomas Clifford. Tradition states that several of his best-known poems, including "The Hind and the Panther" were composed at Ugbrooke, and a beech avenue is still called 'Dryden's Walk'. If we add to all this the fact that the northern road skirting the park also leads to lovely Ideford, then the attractions of Chudleigh and its surroundings have been made quite plain.

A mazy lane leads north from Chudleigh and, allowing for that inevitable zig-zag journeying expected of Devon explorers, finds its way to Trusham—lovely little church and curious painted monuments—and out again to Higher and Lower Ashton; and out *again* to Doddiscombsleigh which, very suitably, lies in a combe under Haldon. This is a pretty place, all cob and thatch, disfigured only by the iron railings round the war memorial. Most war memorials are hideous, anyway. The tiny village typifies the 'approach to Dartmoor' feeling mentioned earlier in this chapter. Here, there are none of the signs of the struggle for survival that all true Dartmoor villages exhibit—proud battle scars. Yet, you know that you are on the fringes. The spirit of the great wilderness broods—unseen, unheard; yet *felt*. Here, under the moorland heights, is rural peace. A delightful granite church, simple, small and enchanting: an imported bit of Dartmoor itself. Its medieval glass is said to be among Devon's very best and escaped the furies of the Civil War only because the village was—and is—so far off the beaten track. There was a thriving wool trade here and the fine furnishings came out of the profits. Yet, though medieval and Tudor wealth brought beauty which the Puritans overlooked, the Victorians got to work with a will and managed to ruin the rood screen. The best-known building in Doddiscombsleigh is undoubtedly the Nobody Inn. "Everybody," it has been well said, "knows the 'Nobody'." A wonderful old pub with a huge granite fireplace: good food, extremely comfortable, gentle lighting, a true village inn atmosphere.

But all this area is a magic land. On both sides of the Chudleigh-Doddiscombsleigh lane and of the roughly parallel B3193 secret villages await the serious explorer. Where the Teign cuts between Haldon and the Dartmoor foothills, Christow stretches an over-long length. It is a surprising mixture of the old and new. The old is very good. The new varies from rank bad to undistinguished. The place began to straggle in Victorian times and lost its shape between the wars. The church—dedicated, as the village name suggests, to St Christina—has some good bench-ends, some good pews and a fine granite tower. Yet it somehow misses fire, partaking of the latter-day blight. But all around there is splendid scenery, especially up on the heights near the reservoirs that supply Torquay, while the industrial archaeologist can find abundant material in the relics of past mining—silver, lead, manganese and copper.

A little to the north but still west of the Teign stands Bridford. The parish contains much beautiful scenery and the village has many fine moorstone houses. 'Moorstone' is the term applied to surface granite. There was a lot of mining round here, too, and the granite quarries and barytes mines were of particular importance. The church has retained an unusual number of its early fittings and a particularly lovely, coloured rood screen. The Henry VIII–Catherine of Aragon emblems appear here, as in several other

South Devon churches. Churchwardens or parsons seem to have been a bit quick to express their loyalty and devotion in this particular case. There was egg on their faces afterwards.

Bridford is the highest of the Teign valley villages: parts of the parish, indeed, top the thousand-foot contour, a feature that gives it a genuine moorland feel, though comparative proximity to Exeter has led to some not very happy development of the lovely old cottages. Bell's *Pocket Guide* (1929) recommended the traveller "to visit Bridford on foot from the main road". This is advice that few would follow in these days, when a walk of a mile and a half seems excessive. Forty years or so ago, the lane was a good deal narrower than it is now, widening for motor traffic—especially coaches—having done much to destroy hedgerow beauty while facilitating access.

Where the Teign valley fishtails, the western fork running through deep woodlands, the northern flowing through more open country, Dunsford stands on a little rise in between the two waters. Although within easy commuter distance of Exeter, the village has not lost its sleepy look. Nor, happily, is it without indigenous resources. Beside the leat that used to supply power for the old mill, garden tools and agricultural implements are manufactured by Morris Tools, a small concern, once typical of Devon, that has managed to survive and to maintain the highest standards while atrophy has overtaken so many local industries.

There is, too, good farming land round Dunsford. The thin sour soil of Dartmoor seems miles away and granite is little in evidence. The old toll road that once ran through this pleasant spot crossed a countryside in which life passed quietly enough for the generations that came and went.

And nowhere in the county—though not always quietly—have more recorded generations come and gone than at Great Fulford, in this parish. The Fulford monuments in what is an otherwise not particularly distinguished church are a vivid reminder of a family that can claim uninterrupted descent in the male line since the reign of Richard I. Even the Cruwys cannot match this, for they died out in the male line in 1804 and restored their name by royal licence conferring this privilege upon the son of George Sharland and Harriet Cruwys. In any case, they cannot prove descent further back than John!

Most of the really old Devon families—I use the term in its conventional sense, ignoring for a moment the biological antiquity of all families—have made no great stir in the world, troubling it little and allowing it to trouble them even less. The Fulfords, however, seem to have had a taste for military affairs—they also had a taste for pictures—culminating in Fairfax's bombardment of the house when it was garrisoned for the King in December 1645. Honourable surrender was very sensibly arranged before much damage was done to either side. That Civil War bombardment, however curtailed, seems an incongruous memory for such a smiling countryside to hold. No visitor can ever forget Dunsford's cob and thatch or the superb views that it affords across what many would regard as 'typical' Devonshire landscape.

From Dunsford there is a choice of routes—either west along the lanes to Drewsteignton, or south to the B3212 and so through Doccombe to Moretonhampstead. Doccombe—it probably took its name from the 'Dogge Brooke' in whose combe it lies—preserves its charm wonderfully, despite the traffic that now passes through the village. A lot of thatch and pleasant cottage gardens, an old trackway up over Mardon Down—from which blessed spot the bold heights of central Dartmoor seem near at hand—memories of one of Becket's assassins, that unhappy William de Tracey whose ghost haunts so much of Devon—all these features make Doccombe a memorable spot. It loomed large in Tracey's mind when, dying in Italy, he left it to Christ Church Priory of Canterbury "for the love of God, the salvation of his soul and of his ancestors, and for the love of the blessed Thomas, Archbishop and Martyr".

From Doccombe to Drewsteignton delightful walks can be planned, offering striking contrasts between bare upland and the wooded splendours of the Teign. Drewsteignton sits on a ridge above the valley and is notable for a variety of natural and man-made features. Fingle Bridge, deep in the woods, is a renowned beauty spot overlooked from a bare hillside by Prestonbury Camp, one of the best Iron Age fortresses in Devon. West of the village, but still in the parish, Spinsters' Rock ante-dates Prestonbury by many a century. It is a very remarkable cromlech which gave its name to nearby Shilstone Farm (the 'shilstone' or capstone of the cromlech) and took its own name from the three jolly—and

North Bovey

Bere Ferrers from across the Tavy

Everybody knows the 'Nobody', Doddiscombsleigh

The 'Royal Oak' at Meavy, across the green

(*top*) Morwellham: harbourmaster's house and 'Ship Inn'

(*bottom*) Ponsworthy village, in the heart of Dartmoor

hefty!—spinsters who are traditionally credited with setting up the great granite slabs to while away an idle half hour.

Nor are these Drewsteignton's only claims to fame. It was formerly a great place for cider drinking. On wet days, so an aged man observed, the pub always opened at seven in the morning, and on Sundays a sixty-gallon barrel of cider was tapped for the fourteen men who worked on his father's farm. These same men always drank two quarts before starting the day's work. Here, too, is found a characteristic tenacity that deepens as Dartmoor is approached. One Drewsteignton family still surviving has been represented in the village for the past four hundred years. Sadly, the couple are childless and so the link must be snapped at last.

Old families, a Bronze Age tomb, prodigious drinking—and the last castle to be built in England! Castle Drogo, about a mile away from Drewsteignton church, was started in 1911 and finished in 1930. Built wholly of granite, this astonishing pile (yes, it really is the only word for it!) was designed by Lutyens and was the creation of J. C. Drewe, millionaire founder of the Home and Colonial Stores. Having decided that one of his ancestors came over with Norman William, he looked round for a village connected with his own surname; and thus was Drewsteignton embellished with Castle Drogo. "There is," says Professor Hoskins, "no comparable house in England."

It is a pleasing thought that at two extremities of this pre-Dartmoor crescent there are two villages each with an inn that does them credit. At the north-western extremity Drewsteignton has the 'Drewe Arms'—the name Drewe having ousted the much older name of Ponsford, a family the members of which, after four hundred years of supremacy, gambled themselves out of house and home to end as a collection of gravestones in the churchyard. At the south-eastern extremity, at Chudleigh Knighton, the seventeenth-century 'Claycutters' Arms' has acquired a justified reputation for food and drink. This, once a cider house for the clay workers and associated with romantic stories of royal fugitives in Civil War days, has now been thoroughly renovated and extended to include three adjacent cottages.

Although some of the villages in the 'pre-Dartmoor' wedge just described lie within the boundary of the National Park, a good

H

case can be argued for the proposition that Dartmoor begins at Moretonhampstead and is fringed by the A382 running south-east to north-west through that delectable place. And even then, this is foothill land. The austere glories of Dartmoor proper do not begin for another three miles or so along the B3212. Then, indeed, a unique region opens up: the great granite upland where such houses as there are seem to be a continuation of the bedrock from which they are made. Here, the villages must seek the shelter of the valleys, for the heights are lashed by the western gales, the rainfall often exceeds ninety inches, and in winter when the lowland roads are clear, snow is driving across the moor and that superb highway 'up over' is a slippery, slithery surface to be traversed only by the foolhardy or by those who must.

The moorland tops are bare except for the recent, and usually hideous, afforestation; but the rough grazing of the moor plays a vital part in the economy of the peripheral farms. It's a hardy land and a hard life. Tin mining and marginal farming make up the past of Dartmoor. Marginal farming and tourism are what its people live on now.

For the true lover of Dartmoor there are a dozen different 'gateways' to his promised land. Moretonhampstead must be high on the list of favourite places. There is a particular sense in which it epitomizes the enduring qualities of the area; it is a haven of light, warmth and shelter when the moor itself is shrouded in mist or buffeted by storm. Perhaps civic pride may be hurt at its inclusion as a 'village', for it has known great days of markets and fairs. There was a time—1801—when the occupations of its inhabitants were given as: "in agriculture, 289; in manufacture, 599". Yet its population today is well within our village limit and it is only in the most technical sense of the word a 'town'. Besides, it would be quite impossible to omit so charming a place.

Seen from the Exeter road, a dozen twists and turns now revealing now obscuring it, St Andrew's stands in a dominating position on the crest of its hill, the tofts and crofts to the west. It is a fine granite church, overlooking its Sentry ('Sanctuary') Field. The present church is fifteenth century, but there was certainly a Norman—and very probably a Saxon—church on this same site. The Saxons were here early in their settlement of Devon, for they saw the strategic importance of the place. In Prebendary Boggis's book *I Remember* there is a vivid recollection of ecclesiastical decay in the late nineteenth century:

He [the Rector of Moretonhampstead] is 75, has been blind for 14 years and knows little or nothing that goes on in the parish, but occasionally goes to church on Sunday morning and recites the opening prayers of the Communion and the Ten Commandments. He draws £900 a year and has a good rectory house and pays the curate a small stipend to do all the work. The church has a west gallery with a golden-piped organ; the mixed choir sit up there, and the men sing with hands in trouser-pockets; under are the school children, and the sexton or verger has a wand with which he chastens them from time to time.

So did the institution which men had loved fiercely, laboured to establish, died to defend, spent their wool profits to rebuild, fall into its late-Victorian corruption. Better, surely, our own polite indifference to its dogmas, coupled with interest in its fabric and purely social acceptance of its nominal functions?

Those who know Moreton best say that its past comes most vividly alive if one stands with one's back to the door of the drapers in the square. Such few modern accretions as there are in this unspoilt little place cannot there be seen. It is essentially a late medieval and Tudor past that then is recreated. A past that thrived on wool. There was spinning and weaving in the cottages; a mill at the bottom of Lime Street and—later—another on the Bovey Tracey road. There was a market every Saturday; cattle fairs in July, September and November—each on a saint's day—and before Whitsun the 'Great Market'. The shops had little half-doors, with fleeces hung above them.

Even now, the place is well endowed with inns: the 'White Hart', the 'White Horse', the 'Bell', the 'Union', the 'Ring of Bells', the Plymouth Inn. In the great days there were also the 'Golden Lion', the 'Punch Bowl', the London Inn, the 'Red Lion' and the 'Sun'. Drinking, wrestling and wool gave Moreton plenty to do. There was tanning, tallow chandling and rope-making, too. And on the upper floor of every inn was one long 'dormitory' where the guests and drunks slept hugger-mugger.

Perhaps the most picturesque part of Moreton is Cross Street, towards the end of which is the beautiful Cross Tree House, once the London Inn, later the 'Courtenay Arms', and now the doctor's house. It takes its name from a copper beech surrounded by a stone platform. A broken old cross shelters under the tree, which is itself a comparative newcomer having replaced an elm blown down in 1891. The elm was known as 'The Dancing Tree', for a platform was often set up on its pollarded top and there musicians played.

This corner of Moreton, from the square, past the Cross Tree, and on to the beautiful almshouses (1637) is as fine a feature as any Dartmoor village can show. Its loveliness is in strong contrast to the grim and mysterious story of the Jacob's Well Murder, a macabre but well-attested incident of 1836, when the unfortunate Jonathan May met a violent death. The story would seem more in keeping set in Dartmoor's lonely heights.

Moreton's ancient rivalry with Chagford came to a head in the Civil War, when the two villages chose opposite sides. The tale used to be told of a benighted walker who, coming off the moor, met a local inhabitant. Unable to extract any meaningful information from the native, the traveller at last asked in desperation, "Well, then, where have *you* come from?" and received the reply, "Chaggiford, oh Lord!" I believe that story was invented by someone from Moreton.

There really is nothing whatever wrong with Chagford! Indeed, we can well echo Crossing's words: "The air of picturesque informality in its appearance . . . has certainly not altogether vanished." It has achieved remarkable and repeated successes in the 'Britain in Bloom' contest—successes, richly deserved and regrettable only because they led the place to christen itself 'The Floral Gateway to Dartmoor': a silly description. That apart, it really is a delightful village, built round a square with its splendid church on the edge. Look out for the tinners' rabbits on the roof bosses. 'Tin Churches' —Chagford was a stannary town in 1305—often carry this badge of former prosperity, business and conviviality. Tin—wool— market: there in successive stages, were the various elements of Chagford's prosperity. Now, it depends very largely on tourists and its attractions as a retirement home. It sits snugly enough up above the Teign, supports art galleries that have achieved a more than local reputation, caters for the annual influx of visitors and shrugs off the world and the wintry weather. There are many delightful old buildings, notably the 'Three Crowns' with its impressive porch and mullioned windows. Nearby is the hamlet of Holy Street with a fine old mill and lovely Tudor House, and the 'graves of the giants' stand on the hilltops around.

Gidleigh and Throwleigh—the former name means 'Gydda's clearing'; the latter means 'coffin clearing' and probably refers to the tumuli that excited the Saxons' awe—are linked by an ancient way. It is a section of the route that passed through South Zeal and Widecombe, a sailors' path that enabled mariners to travel between Bideford and Dartmouth. The blight of depopulation has struck Gidleigh—it is said that between 1962 and 1972 only one child was born in the village—and here, as in so many Devon villages, particularly the moorland ones, the problem is to provide housing in which such young people as there are can set up homes and rear families. And that, of course, depends on finding work for them. Gidleigh stands nearly a thousand feet up; remote, lovely and increasingly silent. It is near some of the finest and wildest scenery in the whole of the northern moor; the views from Gidleigh Tor are outstanding. The little church is characteristic of Dartmoor sanctuaries and has a lovely Tudor rood screen: granite was used not only for the building but for some of its furnishings too. Gidleigh Castle is more of a fortified manor house than a true castle, but it goes back to 1085 and is of special interest as one of the four moorland castles, though the other three— Lydford, Okehampton and Plympton—were much more important. But this tiny village is not easy to better as a base for exploration, and itself constantly surprises the visitor with unexpected sights. The old well opposite the manorhouse gate is still visible to the discerning eye; there are the remains of the Saxon manor house, built about A.D. 1019 for Earl Godwin of Wessex and his wife Gydda—excavations are still in progress—and down by the Chapel Brook stands an excellent example of an early Saxon church, dated about A.D. 740. Gidleigh Common boasts the largest hut circle on Dartmoor—ninety feet in diameter—and haunted to boot! Horses—sagacious beasts that they are—refuse to pass through it.

Throwleigh—despite the ominous associations of its name— is a joy. It paid venville rent and its inhabitants, in return for certain 'Forest' duties, received "all that may do them good except-ing green oak and venison". (Dartmoor had red deer in those days.) No venville man might pasture more cattle or sheep upon the forest than he could winter, 'in land', on his farm. If he in-fringed that condition then he had to pay for his grazing 'as a strange man'. (Theoretically, this provision is still in force; but no 'strange man' dare enter into Dartmoor controversies!')

Throwleigh is not a showpiece or a tourist centre. Most of the summer visitors are walkers, a fact that helps to explain the un-spoilt air that gives the place such charm. There are, it must be admitted, occasional signs of decay—one or two derelict cot-tages, for example—balanced, however, by some good new build-ings, in granite, on the hilly road leading to the moor. The church has fine features, notably the priest's doorway and the lovely bosses, though marred a little by some high-church clutter. The church house is striking, positioned right by the lych gate; and up the hill a little is a splendid exterior granite staircase, nearly a match for the superb example at South Tawton, though the corru-gated iron roof of the building strikes a note of incongruity. A few eyesores near the Old Forge shop but you can turn your back on these easily enough; and the shop itself is a joy—lobster soup!— and seems to cater for everyone. The pub is a step or two, as they say, out of the village, but very attractive at that. What better occupation than walking to it from Throwleigh in the evening?— good company, good drink—and then back to a comfortable bed.

North of Throwleigh, a cluster of interesting villages—part in-side and part outside the National Park boundary—marks this Dartmoor borderland. South Tawton parish includes Cawsand Beacon and a remarkable list of ancient manors and farms: Oxen-ham, Wickington, North Wyke, West Week, Powlesland, Sess-land. It also includes South Zeal, a most delightful roadside village. The supreme glory of South Tawton is the square cluster in front of the church, where Cross Tree and church house and some fine cottages compose a most beautiful picture. There are some good monuments in the church, as is fitting, for the parish abounds in history. Perhaps the most romantic is the John Oxenham tomb, for he—as every reader of Charles Kingsley (and every Devonian, too) knows—saw the white bird. There's a nice little mystery, too, about the bells in South Tawton church. Six in all, number four proclaims "A. Gooding cast us all six. 1744." But Ambrose Gooding did not. His initials appear on five of the bells and, furthermore, the accounts prove that he was paid for only five. A neat explanation is that number four was the first to be recast and suitably inscribed. Number two, it is thought, did not need recasting, but the inscription on number four had to remain. Ah well, it's the thought that counts! Experts differ over St Andrew's, South Tawton. Hoskins describes it as a handsome building with a particularly good west tower. Yet one who knows Dartmoor well finds it 'depressing', though redeemed by those jolly fertility symbols, the tinners' rabbits. You must see it for yourself and decide. I remember only the symphonic setting in which it strikes the major chords.

South Zeal is a splendid place. It was a roadside settlement on the old coaching route now, praise be, by-passed by the modern main road (A30). The excellent 'Oxenham Arms'—early sixteenth-century granite—featured in Eden Phillpotts' novel *The Beacon* and in Baring-Gould's *John Herring*. It has mystery, as befits a place with such a name. In the wall of one of its rooms stands an obelisk of questionable antiquity and with no discernible function. Was the house built round a standing stone? It was once the manorial 'great house', so almost any story could be true.

When it became an inn it took its name from the most illustrious family in the parish. The Oxenhams came to Oxenham Manor—now a farm house—in the reign of the first Elizabeth. They were famous in many respects but for no other feature so much as for their terrifying white bird. "Here lies John Oxenham, a goodly young man, in whose chamber as he was struggling with the pangs of death a Bird, with a white breast, was seen fluttering about his bed, and so vanished." Such were the words seen on a memorial stone in a monumental mason's workshop in London by one James Howell in the reign of Charles I. Several other white birds were memorialized on other stones in the same shop, and Howell noted them all down. But—and this really *is* mysterious—the stones have never been traced. They are certainly not at South Tawton, where there are several Oxenham monuments.

For three hundred years the white bird appeared whenever Oxenhams were going to die. And not only at the ancestral seat—

at Sidmouth too, in Exeter, even Kensington! Then the family died out, and the white bird with them.

It's the right sort of story for delightful, thatched, bucolic, utterly charming South Zeal. (The 'Z' in the name is typically Devon. It's Sele, really.)

Westward, along that dreadful A30 ('they' promise to improve it!) is Sticklepath. 'Stickle' is derived from the Anglo-Saxon *sticele* which means 'steep'. This is a small and charming village of thatched cottages, cut through by the main road from Exeter to Okehampton. It is to be hoped that the present government's plans just (March 1972) announced for improving this kind of situation will bear fruit. The outstanding feature of Sticklepath is the Finch Brothers' Foundry, now being converted into an industrial archaeology museum. It appeared in a B.B.C.2 competition recently as one of six outstanding projects to preserve our industrial past. Originally a corn mill, then a cloth mill, it was taken over in 1814 by Robert Finch and turned into an edged-tool factory. It produced agricultural and horticultural implements and special tools for the china-clay industry. The machinery was powered by a leat cunningly drawn off from the river Taw. Its celebrated tilt hammers, worked by wheels driven by the leat, are unique in the West Country. It is worth several visits.

Behind the foundry is a Quaker graveyard. This is a most blessed and peaceful spot. Who would not lie here, in this green place, soothed by the sound of many waters?

If the present plans to by-pass communities are carried out, then Sticklepath will revert to its own particular brand of peaceful beauty. Meanwhile, it's well worth braving the traffic to see it.

Bear left-handed off the main road from Sticklepath and you come to Belstone, described by one Dartmoor enthusiast as "a shock village in a lovely situation", ascribing her mingled delight and dismay to the fact that the little place was 'discovered' late in the nineteenth and early in the twentieth centuries and has never recovered.

The parish is full of interest: Belstone Tor, Belstone Cleave, hut circles, standing stones, blowing houses, miles and miles of wild, wandering moorland. The 'Nine Maidens' is one of those mysterious rings the number of which no man can name:

And now at every Hunter's Moon
That haggard cirque of stones so still
Awakens to immortal thrill. . . .

As to the name—Belstone—despite all the attractive Hammer-film-type interpretations, there is little doubt that it derives from a fine logan (rocking) stone that "rolled like a ship in a gale". The stone, we are told, has now been thrown down and broken up by quarrymen. Personally, I find the 'official' interpretation just as hard to swallow as the unofficial one that links Bel to the Phoenician god. And *that* takes some swallowing.

There are wonderful things round Belstone and *still* some lovely things in the village. The best, without doubt, is the triangular village green, complete with its stocks and hard boulder for the unfortunate victim to sit on, and the old cottages round it. As to the Victorian and later building—let us agree to ignore it: after all, the moor is close at hand.

If one stuck rigidly to the zones described earlier in this book, then Spreyton would figure in Culm Measure land and not in a chapter devoted to Dartmoor. But Tom Cobley has for ever fixed his seal on Spreyton. He and his immortal companions set out from that village on their way to Widecombe Fair. So—always—Spreyton is incontestably linked with Dartmoor.

"Taught the children a new song: *The Child's First Grief* . . ." such is the entry in the Spreyton School Log Book under the date 19th January 1877. Since that date also contains the entry, "Closed School for the week," we may hope that those children of long ago found some antidote to their sorrow. To read through these log books is to gain an insight into an age which seems so very remote from our present concerns, and, indeed, values.

"24 May 1909. Today, being Empire Day, the Rev. H. P. Knapton visited this school and lectured the children on the 'British Empire'. Miss Knapton very kindly presented each child with a bag of sweets." In that same month the diarist—headmistress of the school—was sending some of those same inheritors of Empire home for having "filthy" heads or for "nasty rashes" (probably a euphemism for ringworm or impetigo).

What a world away it all seems. And how Spreyton has changed. By no means entirely for the worse; though one regrets the long-gone bakers and smiths and the indigenous life. Ironical, too, that the same forces decreeing celebration of 'Empire' should be those that centralized capital and broke up village life.

Now, Spreyton is a pleasant enough part-agricultural, part-commuter village. I sometimes think that it must be the most haunted place in Devon. I've never come across so many ghosts in such a small area. A phantom boy that appears by a bedside; a kneeling monk in the vicarage (very appropriate); a lady in black looking for money; a little boy in blue; an old woman seeking her son. And, of course, the lovely old Tom Cobley Inn from which the immortal ride began; and the beautiful Cobley Cottage, nearly opposite, where good talk and local history still flourish. The fertility sign of the 'Three Rabbits' is carved in the church; and in the graveyard Thomas Cobley, "gent, of Butsford", is buried. He was the famous Tom Cobley's nephew and became Uncle Tom's heir when the old man disinherited his son for being too free with too many girls. Ungratefully, the nephew did not trouble to mark his rich uncle's grave.

South of Moretonhampstead, are some of Dartmoor's best villages. North Bovey must be a favourite with all who know this magic land. Neither tarted up for the tourist nor ruined by the developer, North Bovey is off the beaten track, accessible only through a network of narrow lanes. But it has lost its heart. The village school closed long ago; it has no resident parson; the population consists very largely of retired people and week-enders; and, in the summer, visitors seek its excellent pub and use it as a base for exploring an interesting and beautiful area. It centres on a lovely green. Thatched cottages abound. The green was once known as 'the playstow' (play-place)—and so it was. Here, too, is the old pump. Here—or a little set back—is the 'Ring of Bells'. Here, in short, is Arcadia—if you can get a living.

South-east lies Lustleigh, where, not far from that splendid pub, the 'Cleave', highly competitive village cricket has been played. Now property in the village fetches exorbitant prices and few true villagers remain. Ex-Forces and upper-middle-class retired dominate the place. Soon, you will have to be very well off indeed to live in Lustleigh. This is symptomatic, of course, of the 'Devon Disease'. It was—and is (if one can revalue its function)—a charming village. The Wray Brook flows at its foot. The old houses are grouped mainly round the church. There is a lot of sixteenth- to eighteenth-century domestic building, and all in granite. There is a lot of thatch, too. The church requires a history, not a few lines in a book. But the wonderful pre-Saxon inscription on one of the floor tombstones should be mentioned, even in a book which must hurry on at a rattling pace. Oh, blest are they who can afford to live in lovely Lustleigh! Foreigners outnumber natives, of course.

Manaton lies west of Lustleigh and deserves separate mention if only because part of Grimspound lies within its parish boundary. Nowadays, too, one cannot refrain from mentioning that John Galsworthy lived at Wingstone, again within the parish limits. The T.V. serial having lifted a second-rater to international fame, his connections with an obscure Devon village must be recorded. Manaton is chiefly delightful to the explorer because it is adjacent to so many striking Dartmoor features: Neadon, Bowerman's Nose, Becky Falls—and, most of all, Kitty Jay's grave. This is situated below Hound Tor, at a spot where the three parishes meet. As she was a suicide she was disclaimed by all three. Kitty was an orphan, a poor house drudge of the mid-eighteenth century. Seduced, she was hounded to her death by her righteous employers and hanged herself. She was buried at a crossroads to prevent her 'evil' spirit from rising. Curiously, there are flowers on her grave, winter and summer. Nobody knows who puts them there. This pretty custom had gone on for a long time when a hard-headed rationalist decided to open the grave. "'Twer nought but a daid shep," he said. It was, in fact, the grave of a girl. Some have said that, as human beings rejected her, the pixies took Kitty Jay to their hearts and it is the little folk who bring her flowers.

Here, indeed, is God's Plenty! And yet it is called a wilderness; but all round the perimeter of this wonderful upland there are villages of breath-taking antiquity and beauty. The northern skirts have been explored. For a change, let us drive over the central road that penetrates this magical moorland: take the B3212 south-west out of Moreton and visit the sparse settlements up top.

Postbridge is a comparatively modern village with a charm of its own. It has grown up in the middle of ancient forest holdings and takes its name from the clapper bridge—the finest of its kind on

Dartmoor—spanning the East Dart. There are several of these 'clappers', all constructed in the same way: no arches, but huge granite boulders piled up to form supports for the granite slabs that bridge the gaps between the pillars. Controversy rages about their date, though the balance of archaeological opinion seems in favour of medieval rather than prehistoric construction. Long before the modern road was made a track ran from Tavistock to Moretonhampstead and Chagford, with branches to Ashburton and Widecombe, crossing the East Dart by the clapper and linking the old forest tenements. Both at Postbridge and Two Bridges some cultivation took place and the two hamlets developed first as staging posts and then as tourist centres. A mission chapel opened at Postbridge in 1869; school on weekdays and chapel on Sundays. Both here and at Huccaby, peat fires kept the worshippers warm, and when the Reverend Morris Fuller, who was rector of Lydford and preacher at these chapels, published his sermons— as parsons in those days were prompt to do—he hit upon a wholly appropriate title for his godly addresses: *A Voice in the Wilderness*.

Not far away, Powder Mills Farm, near another clapper, preserves the memory of the Dartmoor gunpowder factory, opened in 1844 by George Frean and employing a hundred men until Nobel invented dynamite. The fine grinding of the ingredients was performed in circular troughs through which huge water-powered stone wheels revolved. The farm buildings incorporate substantial relics of the mills and at the entrance stands a mortar, once used for testing the product.

The whole length of this road abounds in beauty and history. The Warren House Inn, two miles out of Postbridge, used to be on the other side of the road. It was then called 'Newhouse' and was one of the oldest buildings on the moor. Here 'fayther' got salted down. Disposing of a corpse was always a problem in bad weather, burial grounds being so far away. A traveller staying at 'Newhouse' was sufficiently curious to open a large chest in his bedroom and found 'fayther' there, well pickled in salt and awaiting Christian burial. The weather had been bad and the roads 'cledgey-like' for a fortnight since the old man died.

When the inn was renamed it commemorated the warren on which it stood. This was the house in which the warrener lived and

the remains of the artificial burrows and of the old Vitifer Mine—
once one of the richest tin mines on the moor—can still be seen.
Even now, the light of the 'Warren House' is a welcome sight when
the moor is dark and cold. How appropriate, then, the old rhyme
that used to hang outside 'Newhouse':

> John Roberts lives here,
> Sells brandy and beer
> Your spirits to cheer;
> And should you want meat
> To make up the treat,
> There be rabbit to eat.

With the 'Warren House' at one end of a two-mile stretch and Postbridge's East Dart Hotel at the other, what more can the traveller
want?

He will need the comforts of the 'East Dart' to give him courage
to face the Hairy Hand that haunts the road between Postbridge
and Two Bridges. I don't believe a word of it myself, but it was
one of Dartmoor's best ghost stories, the phantom hand special-
izing in wrenching at motor-bike handlebars and rapping at caravan windows. Almost certainly, the camber of the road was bad
and since that was put right the Hairy Hand has had rather a dull
life. It's bound to crop up from time to time, like the Loch Ness
monster. Lonely places cherish their 'Nessies'.

At Two Bridges, again at a two-mile interval, where the Ashbur-
ton-Tavistock road crosses the B3212, is situated the Dartmoor
National Park Information Centre, housed in a caravan. It is open
from April to September.

The Tavistock road runs off west and passes through Merrivale
where there was once a toll gate. There's a pleasant pub, the Dartmoor Inn, a handful of cottages, some old and some newer, built to
house the workers at the Tor Granite Quarries, famous recently
for supplying the stone needed to repair old London Bridge when
it was sold to the Americans. Merrivale was a popular place for
anglers towards the end of the nineteenth century and A. B.
Collier—the well known artist—told a good story about it. He
was having a day's fishing there and happened to be in the Dartmoor Inn when an inquest was being held on an elderly man who
had been drowned in the Walkham. (Inns were frequently used for

inquests.) The foreman of the 'crowner's quest jury' pronounced the following verdict: "Died by the visitation of the Almighty, brought on by crossing the river when it was vlidded."

Merrivale, tiny though it is, makes a pleasant starting point for a day on the Moor. The granite quarry is fascinating and there are some fine prehistoric and medieval remains to be seen in the area. The Tavistock branch of the Abbot's Way passes within half a mile of the bridge and there are two excellent stone rows, sometimes still called the 'Potato Market' or the 'Plague Market' in memory of a time when provisions for plague-stricken Tavistock were left here. There are cairns, hut circles and cromlechs, too, while blowing houses, barrows and some of the finest tors are all within easy reach.

The narrow triangle formed by the Two Bridges-Tavistock and the Two Bridges-Princetown roads contains some of Dartmoor's most interesting tracks and relics and Princetown makes its presence felt from a distance. It is impossible to be fair to Princetown. Architecturally, it has nothing to recommend it, though set in some of Dartmoor's wildest glories. Its terrible prison draws tourists as a magnet draws a pin: coachloads arrive throughout the summer, their occupants gawping in macabre curiosity at those stern granite walls.

Princetown owes its existence to Sir Thomas Tyrwhitt, an enterprising 'reclaimer', who, in 1798, completed the building of Tor Royal, an estate consisting of a house, farm buildings and a plantation. It was he who suggested that a prison for French captives should be built here, and the foundation stone was laid on 20th March 1806. Since Sir Thomas also owned granite quarries he was on to a good thing. The site was given by the Duchy and a small town soon sprang up with the prison as its nucleus: a grim and, fortunately, unusual example of settlement foundation. These were almost boom years for Princetown. There were nearly nine thousand French prisoners inside, quite apart from the large numbers on parole. Many of them had money to spend: prize-money sent from France or counterfeit money which they forged in vast quantities. It was a black day for this bleak place when the Frenchmen left in 1816.

For a time the gaol was used as a naphtha factory, peat cut from Holming Beam being the prime constituent. But the village did not look up again until the convict prison opened in 1850. In the mean-time, Tyrwhitt, go-ahead man that he was, and determined that Princetown should be a success, sponsored the Plymouth-Princetown railway—horse drawn—in 1823, in order to bring in lime, sea-sand, timber and coal and to take out granite and peat. The line was later converted to standard gauge and connected with the Plymouth-Tavistock G.W.R. line. It is closed now, of course, like most of Devon's railways, but makes a superb walk. What Princetown lacks in beauty and interest the surrounding moorland generously provides. Wistman's Wood, the haunted Lych Way, the Abbot's Way (hooded monks have been seen in the vicinity by one acute observer!), Crockern Tor, site of the Stannary Court, Fox Tor Mires, Childe's Tomb, Nuns' Cross and that battlefield called Swincombe are all within a few miles of this grim 'purpose-built' settlement.

The magical moorland road ends at Yelverton, an old name for an old place, though you wouldn't think so. It was 'Ella's ford' or 'elder tree ford' back in 1291. Now, mainly a Plymouth dormitory with a pleasant 'modern' church built in fourteenth-century style, it was called Yelverton when the G.W.R. opened a station there in 1859 and adopted the dialectical pronunciation of 'Elfordtown'. It commands some fine views across the Walkham valley to the north and on a clear day Brentor Chapel, some ten miles away, is clearly visible. Yelverton is 'as flat as a pancake' and, very built-up on either side of its wide-verged roads, it looks rather like a thriving racecourse!

The south and south-eastern arcs of Dartmoor's perimeter contain some of the most interesting villages in Devon. Favouritism is absurd, but Sheepstor and Meavy must be strong contenders for an accolade. 'Sheepstor' doesn't mean what it seems to. The 'Sheep' bit is a corruption of the Celtic *syth* which meant 'steep': and steep it is. Steep, silent, and huge behind the village stands the tor with the largest area of exposed granite on Dartmoor. In contrast, the village is pocket-handkerchief-size, unpretentious, quietly and determinedly fighting its battle for survival. One approach—the main one—is across the Burrator reservoir dam, a dramatic enough entrance to this tranquil place. The wooded valley through which the Meavy flows below the dam abounds in beauty. Sheepstor church is notable for its enigmatic south porch carving where the initials 'J.E.' and the date '1640' perhaps contribute a clue. John Elford was lord of the manor of nearby Longstone in the first half of the seventeenth century. He was chiefly remarkable for having had four wives—a striking example of Johnson's dictum that remarriage illustrates the triumph of hope over experience. One of his wives is buried at Sheepstor and his third—Mary Gale—has a slab at Widecombe. But Sheepstor's greatest surprise is the red Aberdeen granite tomb of James Brooke, Rajah of Sarawak. His nephew—also the Rajah—is buried here, too. What exotics to find in a Dartmoor churchyard! If these are the surprising things, then the feature outstanding for its loveliness is undoubtedly the setting of the village, in the midst of so much natural beauty. And to end on a curious note: Professor Newton, F.R.S., once stated that the sparrow is never seen in Sheepstor. I cannot disprove him, but it is surely a statement that needs checking.

You can get to Meavy quite quickly from Sheepstor, but the best way is on foot, taking what Tony Lumpkin called a "circumbendibus". Circle the magnificent tor, curve round Yellowmead Down, visit the wonderful stone circle (*four* concentric rings), before taking the Meavy lane. Then make straight for the 'Royal Oak' with its carefully supported ancient tree, its wonderful selection of good beer (yes, even today, a *selection!*), its comfort and its welcoming atmosphere. If you can find a better pub I shall be surprised. The fact that Dartmoor can offer several that equal it is a cause of much thanksgiving.

Meavy takes its name from its river; and its river was named before the Saxons came. They—wise men—left it unchanged, for it means 'sea-birds' river'. Farming and mining have kept Meavy going; and now discerning visitors spend a few pounds there without, thank goodness, spoiling the lovely place. The pretty green, the part-Norman church, the atmosphere of Meavy, are part of a very precious heritage.

Southwards, on a combe running down to the Plym valley, stands Shaugh Prior. It was in Domesday but developed in size and wealth through its later connection with Plympton Priory. The large number of hut circles, pounds, ancient tin workings and quarries lying all round the moorland arc suggests a high concentration of population both in prehistoric and medieval times. Now, of course, the Lee Moor china-clay workings and the proposal to flood the valley below Shaugh Prior are distinctive twentieth-century incidents in the age-old environmental controversy.

Shaugh Bridge will perhaps interest more people than Shaugh Prior. There's a fascinating mill (1823) and, of course, the renowned Dewerstone Rock. 'Dewer' means 'Devil'; and look out, for this is one of his well-known Dartmoor haunts. He hunts his Wish Hounds round here and anybody foolish enough to follow will be led to the Dewerstone, over which the whole pack will disappear, followed by their human dupe. There is a nasty drop to the river. Sometimes Dewer reverses the procedure and hunts a human quarry over the rock. One morning the imprint of a naked human foot was found on the edge of the stone; close behind were the tracks of cloven hooves. This is a typical Dartmoor story: a good deal of tradition inventing takes place in the long winter evenings. Bickleigh, just across the river, also abounds in stories—only many of these are true. Benjamin Robert Haydon, that huge-scale and tragic painter, often went there for inspiration. The Slannings bought the manor after the Dissolution: one died in a duel and another was killed for his king at the siege of Bristol:

> The four wheels of Charles's Wain,
> Grenville, Godolphin, Trevanion, Slanning, slain.

(Not that all those four 'wheels' were wrought in Devon.) And in 1798 it passed into the hands of Manneseh Lopes who acquired vast properties hereabouts and rebuilt several churches without doing them much good.

Cornwood and Lutton are twin villages in a huge parish, which was even larger until in 1894 part was hived off to form Ivybridge. Groups of cottages are dotted about the parish as well as farms that were once 'mansions'. There is a good deal of moor in addition to the easier land, but the predominantly agricultural life has now been diluted by Plymouth commuters and china-clay workers. In the tin times, of course, there was a lot of activity here as the ruined blowing houses attest, and tin streaming was carried on even before the Fardel Stone was erected. I have been told that this was the first stone with Ogam characters ever to be found in Eng-

I

land. It was far and away the most interesting object for miles around and has, understandably, been the focal point of many a good Dartmoor story. It is in the British Museum now, very far from home.

Though it looks sleepy enough, Cornwood repays attention. The church has a long story to tell, my favourite incident being the Savery-Rogers quarrel. Savery was convicted of "chiding and brawling in the churchyard" and was forbidden to enter it again until he had publicly begged pardon of Sir John Rogers. This he did on St Bartholomew's Day 1734. Nursing his grievance, he then cut off the pegs on which Sir John and his family were wont to hang their hats. When Dame Mary, her daughter and two servants then used the parclose screen as a hat-stand, Savery prosecuted them before the Archdeacon's Court at Totnes. Sir John had the last word, though. He appealed to the Court of Delegates and Savery was fined £300.

There are many more good stories to hear in Cornwood and, like all these southern Dartmoor villages, its moorland reaches are full of beauty and romance.

If the recent dramatic growth of Ivybridge is ignored then the place can be thought of as a Dartmoor village still. Historically, with the rise of Plymouth, it became the most important bridge town on the southern fringe of the moor; and the old part, centred on the 'ivy-clad bridge' (once just one packhorse wide), retains a vestige of its former charm. The constant stream of traffic along the A38 will soon be diverted from Ivybridge, which is to be by-passed. It was a transit point far back in time, developed with the coming of the railway—Brunel built a wooden viaduct here, the remains of which are still visible—and for twenty years or so was connected with the Redlake china-clay works by a tramway. In 1862 a paper mill—water-powered—was established. It's a pity that the housing estates do so much to rob the village of its former character.

Further east, and much more obviously open to moorland influences, South Brent has more to recommend it. It is often called 'Brent' nowadays, for the need to distinguish it from North Brent disappeared when the latter became known as Brentor. There are two villages—or, rather, one village in two parts—here. The main road has attracted building, but further north the old village sits in a valley with the Dartmoor hills at its back. The hill from which it took its name (*brant* = steep) commands superb views northwards and into the Forest. Before Buckfast Abbey owned Brent, Bronze Age man owned the now-empty moors, dotting them with his tin works, pounds, houses and barrows. When the abbey was despoiled, Sir William Petre became the fortunate owner of the manor.

This was a busy place once. In medieval and Tudor times there were flour and cloth mills. In the nineteenth century it was a famous posting 'town'. The 'Anchor' and the London Inn (Clarence House') were the posting houses and the famous Quicksilver mail travelled this road. Four horses could be changed in forty-five seconds and travellers could be served with a full-course meal in twenty minutes. Ostlers and waiters had to work fast or lose their jobs, for the Quicksilver left Plymouth at eight-thirty in the evening and arrived in London at four o'clock the following afternoon. It averaged eleven miles an hour, *including* stops. There was intense rivalry between the Devonport Mail and the Telegraph, too; but neither could equal Quicksilver.

Brent Fair—held on Brent Down—was a great occasion. The crier proclaimed that "the glove was up [hung out at the Cheape House] and that no man should suffer arrest or molestation until it was down".

Brent church is worth a long visit, recording as it does many centuries of birth and death. There are Saxon remains beneath the vestry and a good deal of Norman work. The six fine bells have ensured a fierce and continuing pride in Brent ringers. They still elect a Lord Chief and a Crier at their annual meeting, still sign their Ringers' Book, still (at least nominally) respect their old rules, and still—this is really the most important point—ring their bells. Now that young people are again taking an interest things have improved, but there are still too many Devon villages in which the bells are silent, apart from a rather dismal Sabbath tolling on one bell. Such a fate is unlikely to overtake the bells of Brent.

Dean Prior, bisected by the infamous A38, was the home of one of the sweetest singers in all English poetry. Here, that man of the town, friend of Ben Jonson, Cavalier wit, company lover, artfully artless artist, Herrick, lived. And here he died. He professed to

hate "this dull Devonshire" but something here excited his
muse:

> Yet justly too I must confess
> I ne'er invented such
> Ennobled numbers for the press
> Than where I loathed so much.

Herrick came to the living in 1629, was ejected for his refusal to
subscribe to the Solemn League and Covenant, returned in 1662
and died in 1674. A stone marks his "assumed last resting place",
and his lovely epitaph for Prudence Baldwin, his 'maid' (housekeeper), whose burial mound is also unknown, has been engraved
on copper by the twentieth-century craftsman, Edward Spencer:

> In this little urn is laid
> Prewdence Baldwin (once my maid)
> From whose happy spark here let
> Spring the purple violet.

Neither the poet nor his maid has need of monuments of brass
or stone.

The east window in the church commemorates him. Part of the
vicarage which he inhabited survives incorporated in a later house.
In the old garden is a bank of snowdrops which, so the present
owners like to think, Herrick himself knew. A happy thought. And
all around are the lovely things that he so beautifully celebrated,
especially the little things: the flowers and the birds, domestic
life. True man of his day he had no use for the barren wilderness.

Buckfastleigh lies in a splendid valley but is, it must be said,
rather a disappointed sort of place. It never got going as the
market town that it might have been because Ashburton always
overshadowed it. It sprang up under the wing of the abbey in the
thirteenth century, to which period the chancel and tower of Holy
Trinity church belong. The nave was a fifteenth-century addition,
by which time its mills were busy. Then, too, there was quarrying,
and the present Dart Bridge (carrying the main road to Plymouth)
was built with local money out of local stone.

For most visitors, Buckfastleigh is simply on the way to Buckfast Abbey. This astonishing place was founded and endowed by

Canute. It perished from unknown causes early in the twelfth century, was refounded in 1134, died again at the Dissolution—despoiled, vandalized and ruined—and rose phoenix-like once more between 1882 and 1932. An abbot was elected again in 1902. Consecration took place in 1932. The tower was completed in 1938. Building still goes on—the new Blessed Sacrament Chapel dates from 1966—and through all these years of continuous creation it is the monks themselves who have carried out the majority of the work. It is they who have raised the stones or carved the wood or pieced together the glass mosaics. A truly remarkable achievement.

Farther into the moor, though surrounded on three sides by wooded valleys, Holne stands in lonely eminence. Just north of the village Holne Chase is bounded by a great loop of the Dart, while its fourth side is terminated by the Two Bridges-Ashburton road. It forms, thus, an 'island' and it has been claimed that 'Holne' is derived from 'holm'. In fact, it comes from *holegn* and could be translated as 'place abounding in holly'.

Just above Holne Bridge iron ore was worked and the discovery in this area of Greek coins of 92 B.C. indicates a considerable pre-Roman importance, just as the old Ram Feast—part of Holne Revels—indicated the survival of pagan customs long into Christian times. In the nineteenth century the Ram Feast was civilized into a ram roasting. No longer did the young men of the village run down a ram on the open moor: the butcher supplied a dead one for the revels. Crossing, that greatest of all Dartmoor men, managed to decipher a curious rhyme on Edward Collins's gravestone. (Collins was landlord of the Church House Inn and died in December 1780.)

> Here lies Poor Old Ned
> On his last Mattrass bed,
> During life he was honest and free;
> He knew well the Chace
> But has now run his Race
> And his name was Collins, d'ye see?

Charles Kingsley was born in the vicarage at Holne in 1819 while his father had temporary charge of the parish, and a window in the church commemorates the fact. It is a pretty little church in which remain, in spite of the efforts of the Victorians, a pulpit and screen dating from the early sixteenth century. The rood loft was 'sacrificed' at the time of the Commonwealth.

The Iron Age 'camp' on the Chase is a fine example of such earthworks, being as near perfectly circular as makes no difference. The superb wilderness of the moorland scenery, the romantic setting and history of Holne, the architectural delights of the Church House Inn, will all ensure the little place its fair share of summer visitors. In winter it is very quiet and certainly at its best. Then, when frost glistens on the Old Dole Stone in the church-yard and on the fantastic hollow yew, when hardly a sound can be heard, and the weight of the brooding moor can be felt—then visit Holne. Test your love of Dartmoor villages when blood is nipt and ways are foul. You will realize then how excellent a site Holne affords for its splendid Outward Bound School.

I have known Dartmoor connoisseurs give the palm to Buck-land-in-the-Moor when selecting their favourite moorland village. This tiny place, seven hundred feet up, where, nearby, the East Webburn joins the West and the newly-married pair hurry to lose themselves in the Dart, is full of charm and colour—such harmoni-ous hues of grey and brown—moorstone colours, moorland col-ours—and all the greens that nature can invent, which means many more than an artist can mix or a film capture.

Since the village received its name many an acre has been won from the moor and many a bare hill has been clothed with trees. Yet it is the blending of moorish wilderness and sylvan delight that, with its human additions of moorstone walls and thatched roofs, gives Buckland so distinctive a character. The little church of St Peter retains some of its twelfth-century work but is mainly fifteenth. Its rood screen is very highly praised. Yet, on the whole I delight to agree with a Dartmoor lover who called St Peter's "charming . . . and comfortable rather than awe-inspiring". It's the compositional effect of the village that is so impressive: that group of cottages by the church, one still a little dishevelled, a bit askew; and the woodland setting lower down, the tidy cots and the cascading stream.

Ponsworthy and Leusden are Buckland's near neighbours. Pons-worthy is a typical bridge settlement sitting astride the West Web-burn. The original bridge was probably a clapper: the present one has a stone in it bearing the date 1666. What the village lacks in recorded history it supplements with legend. Though Widecombe's great storm did no damage here, the Devil himself passed through on that great day. He was riding a coal-black charger and struck fire from the stones as he went over the bridge! Then there was Joey Brown who, returning from the Forest Inn in Hexworthy after a merry evening, fell over some obstacle in a lane on the way home. Fortified with alcohol Joey felt brave enough to tackle anything! And there was no doubt in his mind that this ungainly shape which had crossed his path was the famous 'Black Dog' which haunts lanes all over the moor. Fearlessly he took off his scarf, tied it firmly round the animal's neck and led it back to the village with him where he shut it up in a stable for the night. Next morning, he gathered his friends together and told them of his bravery. He led them wondering to the stable and threw the door open proudly. Inside stood—Farmer Smerdon's old black sow, wearing Joey's scarf!

Well, though heroic deeds like Joey's are no longer in vogue, Ponsworthy is quite unspoilt. All the charm of an ancient farming settlement still remains. Ponsworthy is *real*. And its near neighbour, Leusden ('Leofwine's farm'), over nine hundred feet up, must share in the praise. Hamlet perhaps, rather than village, so we'll get it in under Ponsworthy's wing.

Take the A384 west for a mile or two and come to Poundsgate, a little granite village by the roadside, known to thousands now because of its camping and caravan site—and a marvellous base it is, too. Call at the charming old post office and, for old time's sake, at the Tavistock Inn, for here Old Nick called for his sizzling sup on the night he fetched Widecombe Jan away. The money he flung down to pay his score turned into a handful of dried leaves.

Then on, west still, but off the main road to Huccaby and Hexworthy. 'Crooked bend' they say Huccaby means. Look at the Dart here and it's not so unlikely a tale. It was one of the old Forest tenements and is to this day more notable for its surroundings than for its own pretensions. In fact, it makes none. 'Take me or leave me,' says Huccaby. Its chapel (1868–9) is tiny and dark, and Robert Burnand who once lived at Huccaby House pioneered a systematic inspection of hut circles and stone rows that set the nineteenth century new standards. There really isn't anything else to add except this: go to Huccaby and explore from it.

The most remarkable feature of Hexworthy is Jolly Lane Cot for it is a visible reminder of a once-practised and greatly-valued Dartmoor custom, known as squatting. If a house could be built and land enclosed between sunrise and sunset the builder could enjoy freehold possession. Jolly Lane Cot was built on old Midsummer Day when the farmers—who would have obstructed the work to prevent extra stocking of the moor—were all at the Ram Fair at Holne. The work went merrily: five-foot-thick walls and the roof put on at one end before the walls were complete at the other. (Some poetic licence must be allowed for in such a story. The details must accord with the epic whole.) Tom Satterly, the builder, was an ostler at the Two Bridges Inn and the house was to be the home of Tom and Sally, his 18-year-old bride. Sally outlived Tom by many a year and as late as 1900 was to be seen sitting triumphantly at her door, dressed in a long black skirt, white apron and cap. Well, that is one version. The story sometimes improves with the telling and adds pathetic touches that I have omitted. What seems tolerably certain is that Jolly Lane Cot is the last squatter-built house on Dartmoor.

There was a lot of tin mining all around and the Old Forest Inn was very much a miners' pub. It has been replaced. Hexworthy has known good days and bad. Until Bishop Branscombe took pity on Hexworthy folk, for example, they were compelled to carry their dead to Lydford for burial. How far? "Eight miles in fair weather and fifteen in foul."

It's an interesting place, famous as a moorland centre; but not very happily developed in later days.

Intelligent use of a map enables a visitor to plan a fascinating journey through some well-known Dartmoor villages if he curves north-east from Hexworthy and circles back to the A38.

Widecombe is the most celebrated village of them all, partly owing to the song, partly to its own intrinsic and great merits. There it stands, eight hundred feet up and, indeed, 'in-the-moor'; but, with Hameldown on one side and Honeybag, Bell and Chinkwell on the other, it hugs its east-facing spur above the East Webburn and is sheltered. As sheltered, that is, as any Dartmoor village

Dean Prior, home of Robert Herrick

(*above*) Bridford's magnificent rood screen

(*below*) Thatched cottages at Buckland-in-the-Moor

A long-distance view of Modbury

Challacombe

Lorna Doone Farm, Malmsmead

Bob's chair in the 'Black Venus' at Challacombe

St Petrock's, Parracombe: an unrestored church

Rockford, a street village in North Devon

can hope to be. Widecombe folk 'pick their geese' (you *pick* in Devon, not 'pluck') many times a winter and then snow falls remorsely from leaden skies.

The ordnance map spells it Widecombe; the *Place-Names of Devon* spells it Widdecombe, and explains it as meaning "either withy or wide valley". Crossing thought that it was a corruption of a word meaning 'the sky'—presumably, 'open to the elements'. Whatever the truth about that, it was a great tin centre—Hookney Tor, Blind Tor and Golden Dagger mines. Its noble church—'the cathedral of the moor', to use the cant phrase—was built with 'tin money' and there, on one of the roof bosses, are the tinners' rabbits with their three conjoined ears: alchemical symbol representing tin; and ancient fertility symbol, too—'The Hunt of Venus'. The church tower is considered to be one of the finest in all the West Country, and the impression of warmth, light and loving care that the building conveys is an abiding memory. The satanic obstruction that three times removed the foundation stones from the western site has been thwarted long ago, though a legend attaching to the undoubtedly historical storm of 21st October 1638 (when four people were killed and sixty-two injured during the afternoon service) tells how the Devil visited Widecombe once more, calling for the soul of Widecombe Jan and creating this fearful destruction when making the arrest.

Widecombe Fair is known throughout the English-speaking world. It was a great agricultural event once (cattle, sheep and pony sales) but is now almost wholly a tourist attraction and so popular that those of us who prefer to keep away can do Widecombe no harm. The little place has a wonderful resilience and recovers quite remarkably from 'the season'. Six people live in the heart of the village during the winter, according to the churchwarden, who himself lives very much in its heart, his home being part of the sixteenth-century church house—owned by the National Trust—the rest serving as a village hall. Outside, a nice touch, one of the old beams makes a bench on which Widecombe people can sit and watch the world go by. And here, out of season, I would gladly join them.

Haytor Vale is a 'modern' village, for most of the houses were built in 1825 for workers in the nearby quarries. Very famous in their day, these granite workings supplied the stone for the British

Museum and the National Gallery. Here, too, was the granite tramway connecting with the Stover Canal. What was the miners' tavern and lodging house has become the admirable Rock Inn—open fires, great comfort; a superb base for a Dartmoor weekend.

At Ilsington, south-east of Haytor Vale, the three jolly rabbits make another appearance. Wool was already thriving here when tin also boomed, and between them the two industries made the village hum and the church blossom. At Bagtor, well out of the village but in the parish, John Ford was born. He was baptized in St Michael's on 12th April 1586. Bagtor House itself is late seventeenth-century but Professor Hoskins considers that the moorland farmhouse nearby may well have been the actual birthplace of that powerful writer whose plays, if first produced today, would undoubtedly raise storms of protest from our self-appointed guardians of public morality. Those 'folded arms' and that 'melancholy hat' were often seen when the great man returned on holiday from London.

Ilsington has the air of being a used sort of village with a life of its own. The church stands smack in the centre, a little obviously aware perhaps that Edward VI granted the advowson and rectorial tithes to the Dean and Canons of the Chapel Royal, Windsor, in whose gift the living yet remains. The followers of Aelfstan set up a goodly heritage here when they carved Ilsington out of the waste twelve hundred years ago.

Dartmoor 'quarters' very neatly, and devotees of the villages of one quarter are prone to champion them against all others. Whether eastern Dartmoor villages are superior to those on the western fringes (or, indeed, whether the southern settlements are better than the northern) is not an argument into which a foreigner may fitly enter. It is enough to say that, with a few exceptions, those in the west and north are smaller and bleaker—but not necessarily 'worsened' by those qualities.

One of the most interesting features of Walkhampton is its name. It stands close to the river Walkham or 'Walla's cwm'. The valley, in fact, belonged to and was inhabited by the Wealas ('foreigners', as the Saxons called the Celts) and remained partly in their possession as the Saxons settled in and around the *tun*.

High up on the common there is abundant evidence of an even earlier settlement, for the area is especially rich in Bronze and Iron Age relics. The tin of the moor was streamed in prehistoric times, and there are several blowing house ruins to mark the intensive exploitation that went on from Tudor days down to 1850 when the deposits were exhausted.

Walkhampton itself is a small village centre of a large parish. The church stands on a hill above, its tower a landmark for miles around. The Walkham runs through the valley below the village, which is bisected by the little Black Brook. The old church house has been converted into cottages and though there is nothing of any great note in either the architecture or the history of the village its position and atmosphere manage to convey warm friendliness.

Horrabridge is *horebrigge* or 'boundary bridge', its only really splendid feature being the old bridge over the Walkham which marks the boundary of three parishes. It must have been a pleasant bridge village once, but it is commuter land and a service-housing area now. The 'Leaping Salmon' is immensely popular and epitomises modern Horrabridge.

North-east and on the edge of the moor is Sampford Spiney. This is one of the many areas of Dartmoor where the Devil's apron broke and let fall a great clitter of granite boulders. The church has the typical pinnacled tower, a feature the aesthetic appeal of which depends entirely upon proportion, not only of the individual pinnacles but also on the relationship between the pinnacles as a group and the shape of the tower. There are two unusual monuments in the churchyard: a granite boulder with a birdbath in the top, and a sort of 'hut' tomb. Neither is beautiful, but at least the former is useful. The chief feature in Sampford Spiney is the number of ancient farmhouses in the parish. Professor Hoskins selects Warne's Kitchen (1600) as one of the best examples to be found of the old Dartmoor type of farmhouse with direct communication between living-room and shippon.

As a village, Whitchurch is in a precarious position and will not perhaps maintain a separate existence for much longer. All along the old main road to Tavistock modern development is busy linking village with town—filling the gaps which the Victorians left. But there is a pleasant grouping of pub, church and cottages on the hilly road up to the Down. The old church house provided a resting place for travellers to Tavistock Abbey, for here various moorland tracks converged, notably the Abbots' Way. The priory is a nineteenth-century building but it incorporates a fourteenth-century entrance tower, and the parish has some fine old houses as well as the famous 'blowing stone', used as a sort of sounding board to amplify the horn that summoned the forest tenants to assist with the drifts.

Peter Tavy and Mary Tavy are brother-and-sister villages whose relationship has not always been marked by family love. It would be very hard to improve on Crossing's description of Peter Tavy: "A quiet little place, with a church embosomed in trees, a chapel, a school and a small inn." Written in 1909, those words even now require little amendment. The church, unfortunately, was savaged by the Victorians. The inn is early seventeenth-century, most welcoming, and a good place to hear Dartmoor stories. Sitting by the large open fireplace, the visitor will be regaled with endless moor tales, the latest of which concerns the exploits of the 'Mad Axe Man' who often drank there. Stephen's Grave, by the track leading to the moor, was a suicide's burial place. Stephen killed himself for love and, in accordance with the barbarous custom of the day, was buried without funeral rites, a stake through his heart. He haunted the spot until an especially powerful priest exorcised him during a tempest.

Mary Tavy is much bigger: an old village and a new. The old part is situated where the track from Peter Tavy fords the river. The new part lies along the A386. The Devon County Development Plan envisages the expansion of Mary Tavy (once a prosperous mining village), derelict land, now an eyesore, being used for building. In this far western zone of its enormous territory, Devon—conscious of the scourge of rural depopulation—sees Mary Tavy as a 'key settlement'. Copper mining was the basis of its past prosperity, and the drive and ingenuity of John Taylor— he constructed the Tavistock canal and built the Wheal Friendship leat—manifested themselves very early in life. At 19 he became manager at Wheal Friendship and he was 21 when he built the stone aqueduct for his leat. Not only was he an engineer of genius but he was also largely self-taught. Mary Tavy is a mecca for students of industrial archaeology. Among many remarkable relics it possesses the best-known engine house in Devon: Wheal Betsy. This did the pumping for the Prince Arthur Consols mine which produced lead, silver and zinc.

But all who delight to honour a great man's memory will want to visit Mary Tavy, for here is buried William Crossing, founder of our Dartmoor learning and inspirer of thousands who love the moor.

North of Mary Tavy the road climbs high over the grim shoulder of Gibbet Hill, highest point on Black Down where Iron Cage Gate reminds the traveller of Dartmoor's turbulent past. Here, Crossing said, footpads were locked in a cage and left to die.

Westwards, 'St Michael of the Rocks' stands on its astonishing volcanic height: "a church, full bleak, and weather beaten, all alone as it were forsaken, whose churchyard doth hardly afford depth of earth to bury the dead; yet doubtless they rest as securely as in sumptuous St Peter's, until the day of doom". North Brentor, a mile to the north-east of this remarkable church, has a church of its own. Yet this little cluster of wind-swept houses seems to live in the shadow of the rocky St Michael's, which truly dominates the lonely scene. Like many another hamlet hereabouts, it lives too in the shadow of the past: the shadow of a precarious mining prosperity—manganese chiefly—that, between 1815 and 1860, brought work and people to tiny places such as Lifton, Coryton, Stowford and Lewtrenchard. At the first sign of diminishing profits the money that held the mines together was withdrawn and, overnight, hundreds were thrown out of work in an area where there was no alternative employment. Of these neighbouring hamlets, the best known is Lewtrenchard which was the Reverend Sabine Baring-Gould's parish for forty-three years. A prolific writer— he published over a hundred books—he was also a collector of the folk songs of Devon. Always pressed for time and money, he wrote too much and too quickly, but he had great talent. I like best to remember his romantic and happy marriage to a Lancashire mill girl. He met her when he was a curate in the north and married her in the face of all the social prejudices, of his day. They had a huge family and the story goes that, coming out of his study one afternoon, the parson-author saw a little girl coming down the stairs.

"You do look nice, my dear, in your pretty frock," he said,

vaguely recalling that a children's party was in train. "Whose little girl are you?"

"Yours, papa," she answered, and burst into tears.

The four ancient boroughs of Devon were Exeter, Barnstaple, Totnes and . . . Lydford! Yes, Lydford; though it hardly seems possible now. It owed its importance purely to its strategic position. Its great natural strength made it a key point when the Saxons faced the Wealas and, later, when the 'West Welsh' of Cornwall formed   sporadic, and unnatural, alliances with the marauding Danes. Later, its castle became the stannary prison, and a most unsavoury reputation it had. William Browne of Tavistock (1590–1643) wrote:

> I oft have heard of Lydford law,
> How in the morn they hang and draw
> And sit in judgement after.

The last execution there took place in 1650—the wretch was hanged in chains, his body daubed with pitch to preserve the hideous 'example' as long as possible.

The whole of the Forest of Dartmoor lies in Lydford parish, which is the largest in England; and until Bishop Branscombe's merciful day, every corpse from all the ancient tenements was brought here for burial. Ghostly little parties bore their melancholy burdens over the rough route known to this day as the Lych Way.

It's hard to believe that this little place once had a royal mint; though down in the spectacular gorge it is not difficult for the imagination to re-people the woods with that savage band, the Gubbins, wild and red-bearded, who terrorized the neighbourhood four hundred years ago. Inbreeding and intemperance wiped them out.

The considerable ruins of the castle are eerie, even on a summer's day. Judge Jeffreys—very suitably disguised as a black pig—is only one of its several ghosts.

But there is good cheer at Lydford, too, as well as superb scenery. 'The Castle' (once known as the 'White Horse') is a pub worth travelling miles to eat and drink in. The ghosts seem harmless enough when the fire is blazing and the company is snug on a winter's evening.

The neighbouring parishes of Bridestowe and Sourton are the most northerly of these western Dartmoor settlements. Up on the moor itself they shared a common 'in common' and the benevolent influence of St Brigid, whose 'holy place' Bridestowe is, managed to compose the differences that so tricky an arrangement inevitably generated. The Victorians, in Professor Hoskins' vivid phrase, "practically disembowelled" the once-handsome church at Bridestowe (pronounced 'Briddistow', by the way!) and the twentieth century sends traffic roaring through the little village. Poor St Brigid: she's had a raw deal! There are some fine houses in the parish and, in Burley Wood, poised over the river, a fortification of immense strength. Since the manor was in the hands of the Pomerai family—Norman magnates—the best guess is that this was a motte and bailey erected by them to protect their western empire.

Sourton church is one of several said to have been built by Tracey in a vain attempt to expiate the sin of Becket's murder. The present dedication to St Thomas à Becket is certainly not the original, a fact which lends some probability to the story. The village prospered briefly on nineteenth-century mining. Like Bridestowe it is now mainly agricultural, though the exterior of the 'Highwayman', which has to be seen to be believed, is no doubt intended to attract tourists. There are, however, some pleasing and dignified cottages and a nice-looking restaurant at the foot of the hill. A most unusual activity—which didn't last long—was the ice works. Spring water was fed into tanks, allowed to freeze and then stored in peat-insulated tanks until required. Ice is one commodity that Dartmoor can produce without any trouble at all, but Sourton ice, as they say, didn't travel!

Not only was the Tamar for centuries a national frontier (and still, as Plymouth has learnt to its cost, the county boundary with Cornwall), its valley was also the source of great mineral wealth. Nowadays, that industrial past is being rediscovered. The pioneering work of Frank Booker, backed by the energy and enterprise of the Dartington Amenity Research Trust and coinciding with a nation-wide discovery that industrial archaeology is a fascinating study, has awakened Devonians and others to the realization that the county used to be known for more than holidays and cream and cider. Such a development is welcome to those of us who fear a growing and dangerous dependence on tourism.

The valley, blessed by favourable topographical, geological and climatic features, has also long been a rich agricultural area, particularly known for specialized horticultural and fruit crops, Though economic circumstances are today less favourable—and Britain's membership of the E.E.C. will present formidable problems—the Tamar Valley is still a good place in which to farm, though—as almost everywhere in Devon—the independent existence of the many small farms is increasingly threatened.

Many miles inland from Tamar's mouth, Lifton stands where the Saxons put it to keep an eye on the Wealas. Its situation was of obvious strategic importance and the kings of Wessex valued it accordingly. A royal manor, it figured in King Alfred's will, and Athelstan held court there in 931. Despite a villainous 'restoration' the church is still of great interest for its memorials—Dynhams and Harrises chiefly—and there are some fine old houses in the parish. It is a biggish village with some nice thatched—originally river-reed thatching—houses at its heart. Launceston has overshadowed its former market, but although its mills are now silent it has a large milk factory. Since the closure of the railway everything comes in and goes out by road and Lifton suffers from traffic blight.

North and west, the county boundary used to take a big slice out of Cornwall and kept Werrington and North Petherwin in Devon. There are sound historical reasons which accounted for this apparent abberation but Cornishmen preferred the old tale that told how the commissioners, befuddled by crafty hospitality at Werrington, wandered miles out of their way before getting back on course. Nowadays the Tamar is the boundary, here as elsewhere, and the Cornishmen have 'won' Werrington and North Petherwin.

Delightful lanes lead through hamlets such as Bradstone and Kelly on a mazy route to Milton Abbot. Part of Tavistock Abbey's estates, this manor was added to the infamous Russell's loot at the dissolution. One of Russell's descendants—by then Duke of Bedford—built a 'cottage' at Endsleigh in 1810 and decorated one of its gables with a statue of the last Abbot of Tavistock, prompted either by a macabre sense of humour or by some muddled kind of notion of making amends. Endsleigh is famous for its gardens.

One of the loveliest and most typical of all these Tamar villages is Sydenham Damerel. The church, beautifully sited, sheltered by trees and adorned by a fine churchyard avenue of Irish yews, has a most beguiling atmosphere: fresh, alive and wholly unspoilt. Farming its good land beside the streams that join the Tamar has always been Sydenham's quiet, fruitful lot, though two copper mines were worked north of the village in the nineteenth century.

North-east to Lamerton or south to Horsebridge? The traveller can't go wrong in this delectable land. Lamerton grew up round its church and manor house, taking its time because there really wasn't any hurry. The lovely old rectory, the priest's house and the church (despite a disastrous fire in 1877) are all worth a visit. Horsebridge is simplicity itself, a handful of houses round a once-busy bridge (the third north from the sea across the Tamar) which was built at the spot where horses used to ford the river. The Capunda mine provided some employment, but most of the workers travelled to the larger mines farther south. The houses are an interesting mixture of agricultural and mining styles. The 'Royal Inn', it is rumoured, was once a convent. If so, it has long ceased to practise austerity. Comfortable and warm, it is a romantic embodiment of the happy atmosphere of Horsebridge itself.

To a group of tiny settlements situated in the crevices of a windy upland, and to the area itself, the name Tavistock Hamlets has been given. The origins of these forgotten places—Millhill, Ottery and Lumburn, for example—were partly agricultural, partly industrial, the need arising in the nineteenth century to house the men who worked the mines and quarries. A student of social and economic history will find fascinating material in this strictly non-tourist area where there is dramatic evidence of the impact of industrial expansion on a rural community.

At the southern extremity of this peculiar land, at a crossroads west of Gunnislake, stands Gulworthy. This little place was once connected with the most astonishing of all episodes in Devon's long industrial history. Its unremarkable church was built in 1859 for the Anglican miners and their families at Devon Great Consols and Bedford United. The full story has been told in Frank Booker's *The Industrial Archaeology of the Tamar Valley* and this

K

is not the place to attempt even a summary. Enough to remind the visitor to Gulworthy that from this area in the mid-nineteenth century came a quarter of the world's copper and, a little later, half the world's arsenic. In 1856 the Duke of Bedford's royalties were £11,376. He received this sum as owner of the land, not having risked one penny of capital. In that same year the miners at Devon Great Consols were paid fourteen shillings a week.

In the Blanchdown Woods numerous relics survive; and what was the mine manager's house is now the famous Horn of Plenty restaurant. The collapse of the mines caused great distress and unemployment. Half the local people lost their jobs and many emigrated, an historical fact explaining why, even today, the village post offices in this area sell an unusually high proportion of air-mail letters.

Morwellham is, of course, the focal point. It was a port long before Devon Great Consols was heard of, serving Tavistock in 1105 when that little town got its market and when Morwell, high on the hill above the harbour, was the abbot's country seat. When the copper was found at Wheal Friendship (near Mary Tavy) that genius John Taylor constructed the Tavistock Canal, and Morwellham's boom years began. But until the discovery of copper at Blanchdown it remained a rural spot—small cottages, walled gardens and a busy quay. Then everything changed: the old buildings were swept away and new quays were built. The river was crowded with shipping. In 1850 the industrial cottages were built and a new incline linked the port with Devon Great Consols railway.

Decline set in by 1859 when Tavistock was linked with Plymouth by rail. The copper thinned away. The arsenic boom was brief. Great Consols closed in 1901, and paddle-wheel steamers bringing excursionists from Plymouth were the only callers. The First World War made Morwellham a ghost village; and in 1920 the Ship Inn—once famous for roast beef and 'old October'—lost its licence.

Now, life is returning. Excavation and renovation have restored the long-forgotten image. The imaginative reconstruction is attracting both casual visitors and serious students in ever-increasing numbers. Tea-rooms, guides, trail leaflets, walks in the woods (carefully controlled) and a most fascinating glimpse of an astonishing chapter of Devon history await the explorer of Morwellham.

Beauty awaits, too, especially in the spring. Close by the lazily-winding river, Morwellham sits on its broad shelf, daffodil-strewn fields on one side, rich green Friesian-dotted water meadows on the other, towering conifer forests behind. See it as I saw it at low tide, one April day. Two riders on the sandbank watering their horses: the sky blue, but flecked with clouds: and up-river, Chimney Rocks sharply etched against the steep valley side.

Not far away, hamlets such as Gawton, Tuckermarsh, Rumleigh and Newquay are also part of the Morwellham story, but access to their industrial relics is for the most part forbidden by ever-encroaching Nature anxious to reclaim the spirit of the land she once lost.

Lower down the river, Weirquay is a riverside hamlet with a good deal of lovely sixteenth-century architecture. Like Morwellham it had its nineteenth-century heyday, mining, smelting and shipping all taking place here. A disastrous flood at the South Tamar Consols mine destroyed the confidence of investors and workers alike, but the smelting works continued to refine imported ore. The development of Tamarside fruit and vegetable growing kept the port busy for a few more years, but in the end the railway (late in arriving in the Bere peninsula) killed the shipping. Now, things are improving, for the river is wide here and the sailing enthusiasts have discovered Weirquay.

Bere Alston is a large mainly Victorian village on the site of a thirteenth-century market borough which began as a mining settlement in Edward I's reign. A not uninteresting history, though one that is hardly apparent to the casual visitor! In the silver days it is said that three thousand people worked in the mines which were the chief source of supply for the kings of England. Mining became important again in the nineteenth century and when that declined, the marketing and despatch of soft fruit and flowers took its place. Black cherries and strawberries were the great speciality of Bere Ferrers parish, in which Bere Alston stands.

Many who know this valley well consider Bere Ferrers its most attractive village. It straggles down a hill towards the Tavy, with a pub, suitably placed, close to the water's edge. The Bere peninsula (a tautology really, for *bir* means 'a spit or point of land') is a fine, undulating country between Tamar and Tavy and Bere Ferrers forms an appropriate climax. Its church is one of the most interesting, the tombs being especially notable; and the stained glass in the east window is alleged to be the oldest in the county except for one or two windows in Exeter Cathedral. The age of that glass killed the famous antiquary Charles Stothard in 1821. He fell from a ladder while making a tracing of some of the designs.

Although Bere Ferrers is much smaller than Bere Alston it claims and maintains precedence. The manor was given to the Ferrers family by Henry II and was the 'capital' of the parish thenceforward. Its incumbent retains the title of 'arch priest' and, even though Bere Alston was a parliamentary borough in 'rotten' times, ecclesiastical supremacy remained with Bere Ferrers.

It is there, at that charming spot, that the Devon villages of the Tamar valley end—for me, at any rate. Though I would love to see the ghost at Milton Combe's splendid pub, the place is too small to be a village. Though Buckland Monachorum is a fascinating place, it is too large to be included here. Though Tamerton Foliot had the unusual distinction of being converted by two Celtic saints—with a follow-up by St Budoc, just to make sure—it will in all probability have lost its identity in Plymouth's onward march by the time these words are in print.

7

Mid-Devon

THE northern boundary of Mid-Devon can be confidently defined. The A361 from Barnstaple to South Molton, and its eastward continuation to the crossing of the Exe at the 'Black Cat', divides Mid-Devon from North Devon. It is a very decisive 'frontier' indeed. Even on a dark night a walker who knows this country well could tell at once whether he was north or south of this highway.

The western boundary is even more definitive, for it is the sea! The border with Cornwall is at Marsland Mouth. From here to Hartland Point, Mid-Devon fronts the Atlantic. Once round the point, the waters of Barnstaple or Bideford Bay (the map-makers are carefully neutral in nomenclature) and the Taw-Torridge estuaries terminate the heavy land. For the descriptive purposes of county planning the North-west Devon Coast is hived off as a sub-area of Mid-Devon, an arrangement not followed here, since the coastal area is in some ways very much a part of Mid-Devon. In any case, the explorer of Devon villages—while being aware of the characteristics of each county 'zone' as a whole—speedily realizes that there are many 'focal points' within each zone from which lines of enquiry radiate. It would not be meaningful for our purposes to cut off the coastal belt as an entity, since it subdivides into areas of deep valley settlements; windy, upland, nucleated villages; sparse moorish 'townships' or—exceptionally—rich-soil land that expressed its own personality in a comfortable and confident 'tofting and crofting' centuries ago.

The eastern border of Mid-Devon has been delineated in Chapter

3. Where the rich red lands of the Exe Basin end, Mid-Devon climbs slowly to its sullen central heights, deeply incised by wooded valleys and probed by the finger of Permian sandstone that stabs westward nearly to Hatherleigh.

In the south, the boundary line is clear enough for the most part: Dartmoor's granite upland is a dramatic contrast that makes the traveller well aware that he had left Mid-Devon behind. West of the moor and north of Lifton, however, Mid-Devon sweeps south and encompasses territory—for example, round Bratton Clovelly and Virginstow—that is unmistakably Culm Measures country.

'Culm Measures country' is the key phrase in any true description and, therefore, any real understanding of Mid-Devon as a whole. Carboniferous though they are, the Culm Measures show so little resemblance to any other rocks of the same family anywhere else in Britain that a special name had to be devised for them. The local word 'Culm' was chosen. It is the name for a soft, sooty coal found here and there in these rocks; and though the deposit occurs irregularly and infrequently and, at least during the years that geologists have employed its name, has been of negligible economic significance, 'Culm' has proved a useful term to describe a bedrock that underlies the largest of the zones into which the county of Devon is divided. The largest, but the least populated in relation to its size: indeed, but for North Devon, *absolutely* the least populated.

The soils that derive from the Culm Measures are heavy clay; poorly drained, rush-bearing, *Molinia* and cotton grass infested. Hard work and an advanced farming technology are required to force a living from these stubborn acres. The small family-farmed agricultural holdings traditional of the area had all the labour they needed in the days when a farmer's children were content with a pittance throughout most of their working lives. Present trends are forcing the small man out. Labour is costly. Advanced farming technology demands larger holdings, bigger and more elaborate machinery—and, therefore, more capital. As it conquers the sour, ill-drained soils it inevitably dispenses with manpower. Mid-Devon is still losing people, though in many areas productivity is increasing. Even so, it is thought that on some of the western measures the only feasible crop for the future is trees—softwoods, of course.

I remember reading in one of A. J. Butcher's excellent articles in *The Western Morning News* a description of the Culm Measures as 'whale-shaped'. I don't know whether he was quoting, but I have used his phrase myself frequently. Whether one looks at the shape of the Culm Measures on a geological map or tries to capture their 'feel' in words, it's a telling description. There is a strange power, a wild remoteness, about this lost land of Mid-Devon, quite different from the wildness of the moorlands. The dramatic scenery occurs at the seaboard, where the cliffs are superb; or in the gigantic and heavily-wooded valleys. But generally the countryside has a brooding beauty of its own, little known to any but natives.

Settlement is very scattered. Isolated farms and tiny hamlets predominate, though there are a few surprisingly large nucleated villages built round fine squares—Northlew, Ashreigney and Bradworthy spring to mind. The countryside is undulating. Patches of moderately fertile land are exceptions in the wet landscape. Mixed farming is the rule. Cob and thatch are the traditional building materials.

A good introduction to Culm Measure country is afforded by the A373 from Tiverton to Witheridge. To travel slowly along this road (known locally and descriptively as 'the long drag') is to experience the contrast between Exe Basin and Culm Measures country, Tiverton being towards the northern extremity of the Exe Basin and Witheridge being well into the Measures. It was along this road some years ago that a stranger, westward-bound, met a postman returning from his rural letter round.

"How long will it take me to reach Witheridge?" asked the stranger.

"Wa-a-a-lk," was the reply.

Thinking himself misunderstood, the visitor repeated his question and got the same incomprehensible answer. Concluding that he had met the village idiot in disguise, he asked no more but set off briskly in the direction of Witheridge.

He had taken twenty paces or so when the postman called after him, "Bout arf an hour."

"Why didn't you tell me that when I asked you?"

"How could I tell 'ow long 'twould take 'ee till I zeed 'ow vast 'ee wa-a-a-lked?"

In telling that story I have no intention of scoring points against Culm Measures folk. Indeed, the honours in that battle of wits go to the native not the foreigner. But there is something about the story that is characteristic of the obdurate land.

Witheridge—'the ridge of the wethers—is a large, well-shaped village, about midway between Tiverton and South Molton. To reach it, 'the long drag' has passed Withleigh, Cruwys Morchard and Nomansland, names and places that spell out the saga of Culm Measures settlement. Withleigh: 'the clearing in the withies'. Once the rich lands had been seized the Saxons moved out into the woodlands and swamps, energetically establishing their *tuns* and *leahs*. (Down the road 'a piece', as they say, is Hensleigh—'Stallion clearing'.) Cruwys Morchard: the significance of 'Cruwys' has been made plain in Chapter 6, but 'Morchard' tells a long story, too. 'Mor' is the Celtic *mawr* ('great') and 'chard' is the Celtic *coed* ('wood'). This was the settlement in the great forest, held by Alexander de Crues in 1242. Nomansland speaks for itself. It was tough country to colonize.

Witheridge was the nucleus of all this activity, the earliest settlement in the district. The land around is still hard to work. Soggy, moorish acres top the seven-hundred-foot mark, though—as their barrows attest—they suited the Bronze Age pastoralists. Witheridge itself, Queen Dart, Bradford Barton, Dart Raffe and Drayford were all named in Domesday, showing how far the Saxons had progressed in this arduous work by the time the Normans came. Then, in the mid-thirteenth century, there was a great leap forward: a weekly market and a three-day fair at midsummer—actually, on the 'eve, feast, and morrow' of St John the Baptist. At late as the last decade of the nineteenth century Witheridge still had two fairs and three big cattle markets every year. It was never on a railway—the whole of this area was bypassed during the boom years—a fact that ensured the continuance of localized shopping, marketing and distribution. The spacious centre of this pleasant village, the 'Angel', the soft brown dunstone of the church, all speak of past prosperity and independence.

Witheridge is roughly in the middle of a huge circle formed by the Tiverton-Crediton road, the B3221 (from Tiverton to South Molton—an alternative route to 'the long drag') and the cross-country road that threads Great Ash and Meshaw moors on its way to Eggesford. In the whole of this territory there are very few places large enough or planned enough to be described as villages.

Chulmleigh and Chawleigh on the far western perimeter of the circle so formed are typical of Mid-Devon in being spacious, well laid-out and, to the eye of a contemporary traveller, astonishingly large in relation to the echoing emptiness of the countryside around. Take the moorland road from the A361 at Blackerton Cross and follow it over the reedy upland. Then turn left through Cheldon and come into Chawleigh through the wooded valley of the Little Dart. This route gives a vivid and representative impression of Mid-Devon's hills and combes. In winter time the lanes are mud-covered. High rainfall and poor drainage sweep water and soil off the fields in a sticky fifty-fifty mixture. Any discomforts are soon forgotten in Chawleigh's delightful surroundings. Well, delightful at the centre, where the cobbled triangle in front of the lovely school and school house obliterates the nastiness of some of the new buildings on the outskirts of this hilltop and street village. Chawleigh's huge churchyard is gay with snowdrops and crocuses in spring, and its beech avenue must surely whisper consolation to the occupants of this peaceful field of death. In the centre, too, is a lovely example of a cob cottage with those rounded corners so typical of this material. The fine church itself reflects fifteenth-century confidence and wealth, when Chawleigh ('calves' clearing') had become a speculative 'village borough'. The gamble failed.

Chulmleigh spreads itself rather grandly over the hilly landscape, occupying many different levels and posing sharp questions to travellers wishing to pass through. It would be a pity not to stop and look around. It has had a very long and far from obscure history. An Anglo-Saxon called Ceolmund cleared it from the woodland. By 1086 it belonged to Sheriff Baldwin. Later, it was Courtenay property. That powerful family made it a borough in 1253 and throughout the Middle Ages it prospered on wool. Its decay began, of course, in the second half of the eighteenth century when the textile industry went north, and by 1800 its wool trade was done. Even so, its markets and cattle fairs kept it going and, being on the old wagon route to Barnstaple, it was an important staging post. Then, in 1830, the turnpike was made along the Taw valley and the old hill road was abandoned. The building of the Exeter-Barnstaple railway (1854) along the same valley was the last straw, for the new cattle and sheep market at Eggesford was then far better placed for trade than Chulmleigh's. (This railway, incidentally, is North and Mid-Devon's last surviving rail-link. It has been sentenced to death several times, but always reprieved. How long it will last is very problematical.)

Such, in brief, is Chulmleigh's story, and this is why, to the passing glance, 'it looks so much bigger than it ought to be'. It was an important place once, serving the varied needs of a vast rural area. Take a good look at the church, at the splendid Barn-staple Inn (1633) or at the many other fine old buildings. They are eloquent in their muteness.

Perhaps the newest venture in Chulmleigh will do something to help. It is a doll factory, established with the aid of a Dartington Trust scheme that seeks to establish light industry in under-developed places. (Lack of opportunity is not a purely foreign disability.) Dolls of all nationalities are made and there is hope of a good export trade. The trouble is that such brave and imaginative ventures can employ comparatively few people. The drift of active workers from the countryside that the repeal of the Corn Laws initiated and that the twentieth century has quickened will, I think, never be reversed. Anything that slows it down is welcome.

Lapford, Morchard Bishop, Woolfardisworthy ('Woolsery') and Poughill ('Poil' or, some say, 'Puff'l) form an eastern perimeter to the Witheridge 'circle'. Go further east and you are dropping down into the Exe Basin again. Lapford was notable for its huge milk factory and for the best ecclesiastical woodwork for miles around. Indeed, few parish churches can surpass it in this respect. The village stands high above the Yeo and is a famous local landmark: "when yew sees Lapford yew knaws where yew'm be to". Mor-chard Bishop, like Chulmleigh, suffered from the new turnpike which took trade and transport off the old road to such an extent that the population of this village halved in seventy years. It is a very pleasant place indeed: no wonder the Bishop of Exeter decided to buy the manor in 1165. And no wonder that the Eastons stayed at the Barton for four centuries: their tombs in the 'Easton aisle' adorn the church as their lovely house (1500) adorns the countryside. There is not a lot to say about Woolfardisworthy and Poughill but each is worth visiting: and do try to get the pronunciation right if you are asking the way!

Rackenford stands at the extreme northern limits of Witheridge's 'orbit'. It is small and high and remote, interesting for the arguments that its name provokes—no two authorities agree about its meaning—for its numerous Domesday estates, and for the 'Stag'. A most visitable pub, full of character. Its nearest neighbour of village size is Knowstone ('Cnut's stone') whose 'Masons' Arms' (built to house the workers who were building the church) has achieved more than local celebrity. Parson Froude held the living (together with that of Molland) in the mid-nineteenth century. He had a most unsavoury reputation while living and a worse one when dead. He drank and hunted and lied and cheated and, so we are told, looked like the Devil himself when he entered the pulpit. However, Prebendary Andrews of Chittlehampton has argued very ably that Froude was by no means as black as he was painted. His enemies, the 'Bible-belt Christians'—rampant in Mid-Devon then—very efficiently smeared his character. He was, on this reckoning, no better and no worse than most of his hunting-parson friends. Blackmore certainly believed the worst of Froude, for he cast him as 'Parson Chowne' in *The Maid of Sker*. It's all very intriguing. They say his ghost rides the lanes at night.

West of Chulmleigh, but still north of the Taw, the 'corridor' between the A361 and the A377—both roads homing in on Barnstaple—begins to narrow. The names ring like the Saxon axes that cleared the Great Wood: King's Nympton, Bishop's Nympton, George Nympton, Chittlehampton, Chittlehamholt, Warkleigh, Satterleigh, Umberleigh . . . what a story they tell! The Nymptons, like the Nymets, show the Saxons colonizing places that had held British shrines or sanctuaries: tiny places in woodland clearings or on the banks of streams. In King's Nympton, a fine old village beautifully sited above the Taw and retaining its early framework, the fifteenth-century wood-carving shows how memories of these events lingered on—unwritten, often unspoken, but transmitted in a 'collective subconscious'. The roof bosses riot with male and female heads. Each of the males is a grotesque with abundant mouth-foliage. The old gods of the shrines moved into the Christian sanctuary after seven hundred years of official proscription. They had never ceased to live in the minds of the forefathers of the men who carved these graven images. No wonder the Puritans wreaked havoc wherever they could, though they mistook their enemy. No wonder the Victorians often cleaned up what lingering traces of the dark gods were left.

All the Nymptons should be visited. George Nympton is a quiet, lovable place and, though Bishop's Nympton cannot rival King's, yet its church and its pub and its fine proportions give great pleasure. Historians will relish its connection with Sir Lewis Pollard, an eminent Tudor lawyer; and nobody can miss the humour in Prince's *Worthies* when he tells how Lady Pollard put a new window in the church showing Sir Lewis kneeling with eleven sons behind him and herself in devotional attitude with eleven daughters behind her. Prince goes on: ". . . his lady, glassing this window in her husband's absence . . . caused one child more than she had then had to be set there; presuming, having had one and twenty already, and usually conceiving at her husband's coming home, that she should have another. Which, inserted in expectation, came to pass in reality." The window, alas, is no longer there and we are left to recognize Lady Pollard's prescience and marvel that it could forecast not only the conception but also the sex of the child.

Romansleigh—the name derives from its dedication to the Celtic St Rumon—is the centre of a hilly parish and is a splendid viewpoint from which to plan Exmoor as well as Mid-Devon explorations.

Most of those who know this part of Mid-Devon well would consider Chittlehampton its finest village. The topography supports the place-name interpretation: 'homestead of the dwellers in the hollow', for it lies in a sheltering cup above which soars the loveliest church tower in the whole of Devon. Dedicated to St Hieritha (or St Urith), a Celtic maiden born in Swimbridge parish but hacked to pieces by the scythes of Chittlehampton men, this wonderful church was originally her shrine. It was completely rebuilt between 1470 and 1520, a period when money for the pious work was plentiful and skill abounding like grace.

The original plan of Chittlehampton is plain to see: a large open square, the church occupying one side. Cobbles, cob, thatch, and the mellow harmony of the lovely stonework, the lych gate, the graveyard grass and trees. There is only one blemish here: the square has been covered with tarmac—yet, as the cottage frontages show, it was surely once cobbled. Monuments inside the church tell of come and gone, and most notably of the Giffards of Brightley, stout royalists. Outside—and now a place of pilgrimage—the grave of Jeremy Thorpe's lovely wife, Caroline, so tragically killed and so truly mourned by Devon. On nearby Codden Hill a memorial stands high above the broadening valley and in sight of the sea: here, in Chittlehampton's peace, she is buried with a Pickard on one side and a Giffard on the other. She keeps company with Devon.

Opposite the church and across the road a modest Wesleyan Chapel of considerable charm (1858) looks slightly askance at its ecclesiastical neighbour. Further along, beyond the pump (where St Urith's Well once was?) stands the Bell Inn, a stone-built pub where the drink and food are excellent. Don't be put off by the slightly forbidding front. Inside, all is sweetness, light and good company. This could be a splendid base for a few days of Mid-Devon exploring.

Chittlehampton used to have seven pubs and a brewery. It also had a poacher who kept three bicycles, using two of them as decoys for gamekeepers and police. It still has a village school *and* still rings the bell to summon its children to their work. Its parson has a deserved reputation for scholarship which, allied with Chittlehampton's fame, attracts serious enquiries from all over the world. And yet, with all these blessings, Chittlehampton has a problem: can it survive economically if it becomes a conservation area? Can it safeguard its inheritance if it does not?

As Barnstaple is neared memories of Barbellion's too-little-read book *The Journal of a Disappointed Man* begin to colour the landscape and the settlements. Born at Barnstaple, he died early, achieving little in those two fields, science and literature, in which he showed such promise. A reading of his one book is a necessary part of west Mid-Devon studies. Codden Hill, with which he had special associations, lies in Bishop's Tawton parish. What was the village is now a suburb of Barnstaple. Landkey, on the other hand, is compulsive viewing: a fine church and some important memorials, notably to the Beaupels—*Beaples* Moor lies far east, near Knowstone, showing how extensive their estates were—and to the Aclands, one of Devon's greatest and most enduring families. They began their long career at Acland Barton in Landkey parish, north of the A361 and, therefore, in North rather than Mid-Devon. But the name of Acland may be found all over the county which has favoured them and to which they have given much.

What were once villages along the southern shores of the Taw have grown and sprawled into amorphous straggles. There is little of the true Mid-Devon atmosphere between the Taw and the Torridge until Newton Tracey is reached. Here is another expiatory church (St Thomas Becket), pleasant outside and ruined within (1868). But if south bank Taw is dull, Instow—*old* Instow, up the hill—compensates. Forget 'the front': explore the church and the little street and enjoy the wonderful views.

Alverdiscott ('Alscott') is rather a hamlet than a village but it has a fine, high, windy church and it is on the way—a long way!—to St Giles-in-the-Wood. In this Taw-Torridge land the full meaning of the term 'scattered settlement' comes home to the traveller. Atherington, to the east, and Yarnscombe are the only places of any size for miles around. Atherington is a hilltop village from which it used to be said, with pardonable exaggeration, you can see the whole of Devon. The church is unusually interesting. It has a rood loft—said to be the only one left in Devon—and it is known that the Chittlehampton carvers worked here. Its bench-ends are so good that they have made some visitors think that they were on the Quantocks instead of in Mid-Devon. The effigies and tombs are remarkable, too. Yarnscombe cannot compete with Atherington ecclesiastically, but its name—'Eagles' combe'—though recalling a species long extinct in Mid-Devon is a reminder that it is situated in an area of totally unspoilt country, right off the beaten track, undiscovered by tourists and a paradise for naturalists.

High Bickington, due south of Atherington, is a hilltop village, like so many others in this sparsely-populated area. Here again, in the church, are bench-ends of a richness and intricacy rare in Devon. The notable feature here—apart from the vividness of the carving—is the span of the centuries: late Gothic, Renaissance and, most unusually, modern.

Roborough—'rough hill'—set in a ring of Domesday farms and manors, and a mile south of the delightful early sixteenth-century Coombe Barton, has a lovely church and, with soggy land to the east and woodland to the west, epitomises in the space of one parish most of Mid-Devon's salient features. Its southern neighbours, Burrington, Riddlecombe and Beaford, are all unspoilt and quiet spots. Burrington—hilltop again—commands superb views. Its church is virtually untouched early sixteenth-century and, again unusually, has a granite arcade and a splendid wagon-roof with angel decorations, incongruously reminiscent of some of the fine churches in the Somerset Levels. Riddlecombe lies lower and some experts believe that its name enshrines the memory of the ford that was once so important in the woods enclosing the nearby Mully Brook, otherwise a considerate abstacle to travellers. Beaford seems to have been famous for its gadflies, while Woolleigh—a Barton in the parish, seventeenth-century, but unhappily modernized—was once 'wolves clearing', a name that reminds us of the distant past when all this land had to be worked or fought or hunted for. Today, Beaford is remarkable for its famous Centre. Established by Dartington Hall Trustees in 1966, this remarkable enterprise sponsored 280 performances all over North and Mid-Devon in 1971, attended by 35,000 people. The contribution that it makes to an area, in so many ways impoverished, cannot be measured in material terms—". . . actors working with children in a school, a brass band concert at Holsworthy, young people making a film, a jazz band in a pub, and, a world away, another audience listening to Bach". That quotation from its report for 1971, the growing confidence of the Orchard Theatre, and the developing local awareness that here is something good—these are remarkable results from a bravely imaginative venture.

Ashreigney, a little to the south, is a superbly planned, square, nucleated, Saxon village. A late nineteenth-century restoration knocked the heart out of its fifteenth-century church, but nothing has yet spoilt that splendid, story-telling village centre. Only bulldozing could. The original lay-out was clear, firm, tight.

Dolton, just south of west, clusters round St Edmund's church, possessor of a remarkable font, decorated with Scandinavian serpent work. 'The Royal Oak' is a mouth-watering and thirst-quenching establishment of great charm, enhanced by its thatched neighbours. A little modern building here, inept as usual; and a bungalow rejoicing in the name of Aljoy!

Iddesleigh is not far from Dolton. Eadwig was a lucky man, though he would not appreciate those views of Dartmoor as we do. A lot of surplus wealth is needed before society can produce people who delight in wilderness. Iddesleigh gives the appearance of being thatchier than anywhere else in Devon. Thatch everywhere. The houses positively sprout. That delectable 'Duke of York' stands back from the road: a narrow street in front, through which nothing but native traffic passes. Then a row of thatched cottages again, and Smithy Road with old farm engines parked just as if some dead farmer had left them waiting while he nipped in for a drink. A tall mast on a little green commemorates the coronation of the bearded George V. It seems completely at home in a pre-1914 village.

The main road south out of Iddesleigh leads to Monkokehampton, a pleasant crossroads hamlet, its rebuilt church standing a little way out of the settlement. The right-hand fork leads to Hatherleigh and here, all the way east to Crediton, that errant tongue of richer land produces surprising results on the landscape. There are miles of lanes hereabouts where on one side you see typical Mid-Devon sparseness and on the other, Red-Land richness. Hatherleigh itself was intended for civic stature, and, indeed, enjoyed it for many a year. There is splendid domestic architecture spanning the sixteenth to early nineteenth centuries and the 'George'—part fifteenth-, part sixteenth-century—was the old court house of Tavistock Abbey. It is delightful outside and in. So, too, is the London Inn, again, in part, fifteenth-century. Hatherleigh suffered a great fire in 1840 and has been hard hit by dwindling population ever since; but what a peaceful, pleasant holiday base it makes! Surprisingly, it has recently been anxious to acquire a coat of arms—it is officially a 'town', not a village. The College of Arms made a search but drew a blank. The only Hatherleigh people entitled to arms seem to have been the Yeos who lived at Passaford centuries ago. At the time of writing, the Hatherleigh Fathers are debating the offer of the College of Arms to cook something up for them at a fee of £400.

Left-handed at Monkokehampton, the road runs along a hilly shoulder into Winkleigh, passing on its outskirts Inch's cider factory. People come from miles around to pick up five-galloners here, braving the rigours of the windiest hill in Devon. Inch's factory supplies a good many pubs, too, with its superb product. It's a wonderfully interesting place and the sight of those hogsheads—six grades from sweet to dry—is a sight to gladden any man's heart. You may think you don't like cider: try Inch's and you'll change your mind. But careful! It's strong, and excellent value for money.

Winkleigh—Wineca cleared the woodland from the hilltop—was a Saxon plantation, part agricultural settlement and part fortified centre. Later, the Normans built a very small castle here. Study of the map shows that this was a commanding situation. For centuries it was an important local centre for goods and services and had both a market and a fair. Decline was rapid after the mid-nineteenth century and its population halved in ninety years. It's the same old story: flight from the land accompanied necessarily by the impoverishment and finally the extinction of butchers and bakers, candlemakers and brewers, tailors and cobblers, coopers and smiths, ropemakers and saddlers, wheelwrights and . . . and. . . . Agricultural implements, tractors and cars are serviced and repaired in Winkleigh today. There are some shops—general stores, provisions, ironmongers; but it's a quiet little place, charmingly grouped round its church which seems a stone island in a sea of cob and thatch. There's a lovely square with the 'King's Arms' on one side and the Winkleigh Hotel on the other, and a very odd-looking elongated pyramid of a pump "erected by permission of the Lord of the Manor", and a parish notice board the contents of which most vividly—and sometimes amusingly—convey the flavour of village life.

Sampford Courtenay, due south of Winkleigh, has a big inn right on the main road, but the village itself lies up a quiet street. Its slender pinnacled church tower is golden with the lichen that grows and flows down the ancient stone. Cobbles pave the street in front of the lych gate and foot the lovely old church house with its worn external stairs. Here, on Whit Sunday 1549, the ill-fated Prayer Book Rebellion began. The new service, said the men of Sampford Courtenay, was "but a Christmas game". The next day,

L

they challenged the secular power by going back to the Latin Mass. The magistrates moved in and William Hellyons was killed on those lovely church house stairs. They joined the Cornishmen and marched off enthusiastically to the siege of Exeter—and to their deaths.

North Tawton, not a particularly attractive-looking place is yet full of interest. The common story of a woollen trade that dwindled away after the mid-eighteenth century and a series of very damaging fires has not left much on the ground to enable the traveller to piece out its history and its former importance. But welcome signs of returning life are in evidence: a large building materials depôt and the busy Water Board headquarters and some bustle down by the square. This little place—its population not yet back to eighteenth-century numbers—was a market 'town' as far back as 1199. Later, it became a borough and elected its portreeve annually until the nineteenth century ended. Although the church has suffered greatly from well-meant 'improvements', one feature will teach the enquiring traveller a lot: compare the few surviving sixteenth-century bench-ends with the stiff and lifeless Victoriana predominating. I would recommend a visit to North Tawton to anyone who wants to understand 'real' Devon today—the years of decline that lie behind; the struggle to survive that is now being waged. To know Devon you must get off the tourist routes and away from the 'honeypots'. Truth compels the statement, yet I hope that few will take the advice!

East of North Tawton lies Bow, now a 'characteristic street village' and illustrating an old historical trend. The Norman Conquest—like it or lump it, and on the whole I prefer to lump!—brought settled conditions to the countryside. Before Norman William's day settlements were often hidden, for security, deep in forest clearings. Once the Conqueror's iron hand had gripped the country, some of these secluded sylvan settlements were abandoned and new sites were found, along the new roads where trade was brisk and where marauders were now rare. Bow is an instance of this process. The old settlement was at Nymet (notice the Celtic influence) Tracey. Indeed, the migration was sufficiently prolonged for the parish church to be built nearer to the old settlement than the new. Finally, as law and order prevailed, Bow grew on both sides of the highway, outstripping its original, which dwindled away to a mere 'church town'. A weekly market and a three-day fair were insufficient to make anything very much of Bow when, early in the fourteenth century, it became a speculative 'borough'. These little places were the 'Poseidons' of the fourteenth and fifteenth century. The speculators were the lords of the manor. They hoped for a quick killing.

Copplestone, in Colebrooke parish, but only just, appears to have derived its name from 'rocking-stone' (Anglo-Saxon), in which case its position, right on the borders of three parishes, was probably marked by a long-forgotten boundary logan. But if its rocking-stone has gone, its marvellous cross endures, twelve feet high, with intricate carvings, marking the boundaries of Colebrooke, Crediton and Down St Mary parishes and said to indicate the place where Putta, Bishop of Devon, was murdered in 905.

From this charming crossroads village it is a short journey to Colebrooke itself, where the church has a fine Perpendicular west tower and some most remarkable bench-ends and woodwork that bear comparison with anything in Devon. And all around are farms and manors that date at least from Domesday and in which the pioneers who opened up this lost land had their habitation.

West of the A386 (from Okehampton to Bideford) we enter what was for a long time debatable land. Here, the Saxons had to inch their way forward to the ultimate frontier. Hatherleigh sits astride this road and so does Great Torrington. The former has been mentioned already; the latter, one of Devon's finest hilltop towns, has too large a population to warrant inclusion here. (But don't fail to visit it.) Black Torrington, its not-so distant neighbour, sits almost on the bank of the Torridge and tends to get written off by the guide-books but is, in fact, well worth a visit, and not least for being the home of that indomitable writer-scholar, Ernest Martin, whose books have given pleasure to all students of West Country life.

Settlement is very sparse round here. Except towards the estuaries, where drainage improves, the Culm Measures get more and more stubborn the further west one goes. Shebbear has a large square and a delightful seventeenth-century New Inn, while its church boasts some fine Norman work. It also houses one of those small 'independent' schools in which Devon abounds. Dr Shebbear—its founder—was an eighteenth-century Noncomformist divine about whom Dr Johnson made a joke. That, in itself, is a kind of immortality.

To the south, Beaworthy and Inwardleigh are good examples of these lost Mid-Devon places. Both were 'worthies'—farms— belonging to Anglo-Saxon Worthies, long-forgotten but that their names (Beaga and Inwar) cling to the map centuries after they became dust. It is through visiting 'undistinguished' places like this that Mid-Devon is felt.

Between them stands Northlew, famed for the Norman work in its church and its later (mainly Tudor) woodwork. One of its windows features four saints, of whom the most interesting is St Brannock, brown-clad and holding a crozier and a spade. The legend is that he pioneered the settlement of west Mid-Devon by clearing woodland and ploughing. It is a wildly unhistorical story, but its moral holds to this day.

Where the Okehampton-Launceston road dips southwards, we enter country that is more obviously 'strategic' land than anywhere else in Devon. To this day, it is almost empty apart from one or two big and important agricultural-military settlements. Their military importance soon dwindled after the Norman Conquest: a transient manufacturing wealth departed round about 1800, at the latest. Agriculture survives—precariously.

Holsworthy is the undisputed centre of this high, windy, yellowy clay land, yet it has been harshly described in many a book. It cannot be said to have picturesque qualities, and for too many years signs of decay were evident. That was not surprising. A 'failed' town takes knocks. In the days of prosperity it had markets and a fair; it was a speculative borough with a portreeve; it reached its greatest importance before 1850 and then went steadily down. It has never had much tourist appeal, so it could not replenish its collective and private coffers in 'the season'. Nowadays, however, things are looking up a bit. It is on the way to Bude and the superb north Cornish coast and makes something out of the transit traffic. It has recovered, too, some of its former importance as a goods and services centre for a huge though struggling area. One of the most encouraging developments of recent years has been the success of Holsworthy Electronics Ltd.

This young and enterprising firm opened in the Holsworthy drill hall in 1967. It manufactures high-quality electronic components and supplies industries as diverse as aircraft, computers and colour-television manufacture. Enterprise such as this deserves every encouragement, for it means new life for dying villages, Though the labour force for each such venture cannot be large, a number of small firms producing goods, light in weight, with a high proportion of skilled labour built into the finished product, could do much to remove the twin blights of depopulation and unemployment that now afflict large areas of Mid and North Devon—and without in any way diminishing their rural attractions.

Between Holsworthy and Lifton (which was taken in Chapter 6 as the northward termination of the Tamar valley settlements) there are several fascinating villages. Highampton, midway between Holsworthy and Hatherleigh, looks out over Dartmoor, the swelling bulk of Cawsand Beacon dominating the southern skyline. Though the church was pulled about twice during the nineteenth century it has retained its splendid Norman doorway and font. Burdon is the most interesting house for miles around, its Tudor remnants bearing the date 1569 and the initials EB: AB—touching relics of a family that lived here for six and a half centuries. Two miles north-east, Totleigh Barton housed Zouches and Fitzwarrens in the twelfth and thirteenth centuries and once had a private chapel dedicated to St Katherine.

Luffincott, very near the Cornish border, is hardly a village, but though its church is of no great interest in itself and no deeds worth putting in any history book were enacted here, it demands mention because its parson disappeared in 1904 and was never seen again. He was neither in financial nor woman trouble. He just walked out of the parsonage one evening—into thin air. Many a time afterwards the sexton followed his spectral form down the churchyard path, called him by name, struggled to catch him up; but never a sign of recognition nor an answering word did he receive.

Pyworthy—like Hopworthy—got its name from some Anglo-Saxon joker. The first element in each means insect or grasshopper, evidently nicknames for the original owners who settled in this not very hospitable land. These were not lonely outposts vulnerable to Celtic attack, but beautifully planned and strategically placed strongholds. Ashwater is a remarkably attractive village clustering round its green, with a most interesting part-Norman church. A Courtenay killed in that bloody struggle at Tewkesbury lies here. Virginstow (the name is self-explanatory) stands high on a ridge and looks far into Cornwall, facing the direction from which danger was feared all those centuries ago.

Germansweek takes its strange name from St Germanus of Auxerre (to whom its church is dedicated) and *wick* meaning 'dairy farm'. It lies hidden in a lost clay land which has not changed all that much since the Saxons made farms where the Celts hardly set foot. Set on a hill overlooking the river Wolf, the little place was obviously a central strong point in a settlement pattern that embraced Southweek, Westweek, Seccombe and Brockscombe, to name only a few of the ancient farms and manors that lie between the Wolf and the Carey.

South again, and nearing the skirts of Dartmoor, is Bratton Clovelly. The best guess at the meaning of Bratton is 'the settlement on the strip of uncultivated land'—an interpretation that gains support from topography, Bratton lying on a hill which itself is part of a ridge between two waters. Clovelly has taken its present form by assimilation with the famous coastal village, but is derived from Clavilles who held the manor in the thirteenth century. Bratton is a very lovely village indeed, both in site and in plan, and its church must be one of the finest in the county. Its interior is of cathedral-like proportions, lofty, colourful, breathtaking. Where *did* the money come from to build this superb edifice in this remote land?

North of Holsworthy the sea begins to call, just as, to the south, the brooding moorland makes its imminence felt. Bradworthy and Woolfardisworthy (yes, another Woolsery!) are the only places of village dimensions between Holsworthy and the coastal settlements, though there are many delightful hamlets—the Putfords, Sutcombe, Abbots Bickington. . . . Bradworthy is one of the most important of all Devon villages from an historical point of view. To this day it shows its original lay-out with perfect clarity. Here, at the far western outposts of Wessex, when the Saxons were pushing the frontier deeper into Wealas land, in the years when the boundary was now the Tamar, now the Ottery, and back to the Tamar again, Bradworthy was established by the fighting farmers in about A.D. 700. It is a perfect sample of the nucleated village; tofts, crofts and back lane; large 'square'; houses clustered round the well; church on one side; and around—though now long-obliterated—the open-field system. A delightful, textbook example of such a place.

Woolfardisworthy lies north, four miles nearer the sea as the crow flies. It is sited high above the marshy ground of which there is so much in this large and lonely parish. It has a very interesting church—excellent bench-ends and the Prust memorials—a good pub and, when times got better, it threw out a charming little offshoot called West Town where there is a fine cluster of old farms and cottages.

From the Cornish border at Marsland Mouth right round to Bideford, in the coastal strip cut off by the A39, there are very few true villages. This land is noted for the works of nature not those of man. Hartland ('stag island', the authorities say, though the huge parish—the extreme north-west tip of Devon—forms a peninsula not an island) contains within its parochial boundaries cliff scenery unsurpassed throughout Britain, and coastal waterfalls equalled only in Scandinavia. The inland scenery is wide and moorish, dotted with isolated whitewashed or grey slate cottages. Bronze Age barrows abound and, apart from the stupendous Iron Age earthworks at Clovelly Dykes, Hartland parish itself contains notable examples of 'cliff castles'.

Hartland, a long, follow-the-lie-of-the-land, street village now, belonged to King Alfred, was left by him to Edward, and stayed with the kings until Canute gave it to Gytha, Harold's mother. William the Norman took it over and the Dynhams had it after him. It stayed with them until 1501 when it was split up between four daughters.

Although it had a market and a fair and became a borough it was too isolated ever to do much more than act as a centre to its immense parish. The best buildings—apart from the church—are of the late eighteenth century, a period when its population was at its height and when its little port was flourishing.

The splendid church was founded by Gytha and dedicated to St Nectan in gratitude for her husband's escape from shipwreck. Originally, it was a collegiate church with twelve canons but nothing much is now left of the abbey except for fragments that were incorporated when the present big house was rebuilt in 1779. St Nectan's today stands high up at Stoke, its tall tower a sea-mark. A whole book could be written about it—screen, bench-ends, priest's chamber—so full of interest and beauty is it. In the summer of 1971 it was the setting for a performance of Ronald Duncan's play *Abelard and Heloise*. Duncan, who lives in Welcombe—Devon's 'last parish'—directed the production, itself the centre-piece of a week-long Hartland arts festival. One of the most heartening features of Mid-Devon village life in recent years has been an upswell of artistic ventures. First signs, some of us like to think, of returning vitality.

Below Stoke, at Hartland Quay, are the remains of a vanished port. Here—for certain—ships came and went for centuries. It seems impossible now. Yet the quay, for which the leading sailors of England petitioned—Raleigh, Drake and Hawkins among them —and which was authorized by an Act of Parliament in 1566, served its purpose until the sea overwhelmed it in 1893. To maintain what was essentially an artificial harbour on this iron, stormy coast was a work requiring great skill and labour. To bring ships in and out demanded nerve and knowledge. Trade reached its peak in the late eighteenth and early nineteenth centuries: malt, barley, wheat and wool went out; timber, coal, guano, slates, limestone, building materials and rope came in.

Now, the harbourmaster's house, the stables and warehouses, are a comfortable hotel; and here the 'Green Ranger' bar epitomizes the long history of Hartland Quay. The name commemorates the daring of the Appledore lifeboat men who, in a gale in November 1962, rescued the crew of the *Green Ranger* (an Admiralty Fleet Auxiliary tanker on tow from Plymouth to Cardiff) which had been driven onto the rocks near Long Peak.

Everybody who has heard of Devon has heard of Clovelly. To many, indeed, it symbolizes all that Devon 'stands for'—sea-dogs, picturesqueness, quaint ways and people. There is an element of truth in this, but only an element. In disputing the holiday-makers' assumptions we intend no disrespect to them and certainly no dispraise of incomparable Clovelly.

It is, as Devon villages go, a 'new' village. Seven generations of the Carys lived at Clovelly between 1457 and 1724, but it was

George Cary (1543–1601) who created the place we know today. An extract from his will makes the point: "I have of late erected a pier and quay . . . and also divers houses, cellars, warehouses and other edifices, as well under the cliff and on the salt shores of Clovelly . . . which standeth and hath cost me about £2,000 and which place was of none or very small benefit before my said exertions and buildings."

George Cary had, in fact, made the only safe harbour between Appledore and Boscastle by his "said exertions and buildings". Now, the fishing industry—the famous Clovelly herring shoals— and the ship-borne trade have waned, but what Edward Capern (Devon's 'postman-poet', born near Tiverton and buried at Heanton Punchardon) called "a village like a waterfall" is one of Devon's most famous beauty-spots, magnet for holidaymakers from all over the world. The visitors of today are the herrings of yesterday.

The little place is just a cleft in the cliffs. Old cottages flank the famous High Street that tumbles precipitously to the quay. There is no internal transport except the donkeys. Her Majesty's Mail comes up that beloved street in panniers.

Clovelly never changes. It is owned by the Clovelly Estate Company which fights to preserve its every feature. Popular in the extreme, Clovelly makes no concessions to popularity, knowing that by remaining itself it preserves its livelihood. Telephone and electricity cables were laid underground: much-needed sewers did not destroy the cobbles—they were relaid by hand, regardless of expense.

Yet depopulation threatens. What is there to keep youth in this showpiece? The estate company and the parish council are alive to the threat, but have so far been thwarted in their attempts to bring in light industry. Clovelly seems doomed to live off tourism and to replace its emigrating youngsters by the immigrant elderly.

The Shrove Tuesday rites at Clovelly are surely unique. At dusk, the children run up and down the precipitous cobbled street towing tin cans on long strings. A deafening din scares off the witches, once the scourge of this remote land. They call it 'Landsherd Night'. (*Land* is a Devonshire word meaning 'to hit'; and 'sherd' has its Biblical sense of 'pots and pans'.) It was not only witches that troubled the neighbourhood. The Greggs—a vast incestuous tribe—lived in a cave near Clovelly and terrorized the neighbourhood for years. Eventually executed, they had for years murdered and robbed and were reputed to practise cannibalism.

Mid-Devon's coastal strip ends northwards in the flat sand lands that flank the southern shores of the Taw-Torridge estuary. Northam, Westward Ho! and Appledore are not really villages any longer. Northam and Westward Ho! are resorts. Appledore— still magical—is part resort, part fishing village, part (thank goodness) a successful, skilful, shipbuilding town.

Abbotsham is the last village on the coastal belt. It once belonged to Tavistock Abbey, a fact enshrined in its name and memorialized in the superb bench-ends in its lovely church. Here, where sea and shore come peacefully together and where the long miles of Mid-Devon's Culm Measures undulate inland, the traveller leaves the villages of the county's isolated, neglected, strangely-beautiful clay belt.

8

North Devon and Exmoor

NORTH of the A361 the Devonian rocks appear again. That road, indeed, follows very closely the dividing line between the Culm Measures and the complex foldings, dips and swells of all three Devonian 'ages' which characterize North Devon, providing geologists with endless interest and unresolved debate. The geological confusions of the area have produced a variety of scene remarkable even in Devon, a county of surprises. Thirty-six miles, at its widest, from west to east, and fourteen miles, at its longest, from north to south, this is a protean land. But a zone that begins in the west with blown sand dunes and ends in the east on Exmoor's windswept plateau must show many different faces to the traveller.

Few descriptive generalizations are possible and, when attempted, have the uncomfortable knack of suggesting the exceptions that test their validity. This is hilly land rolling upwards unevenly but steadily to the open grass moor of western Exmoor, where the uniformity of elevation is frequently broken by precipitous combes. The coast is distinguished by its bold cliffs. The lower valleys are heavily wooded. Beech hedges abound, their rust-red leaves making winter more lovely than summer. Stock rearing is the chief agricultural activity, but tourism is becoming more important every year and many a lonely farm now has its own share of 'the season'. The hamlet, the isolated cottage or barton predominate in the settlement pattern, sheltering themselves in the valleys. Slate is the local building material most commonly used.

That said, it is more helpful to look at four 'sub-districts' into which the North Devon Coast and Exmoor can be divided and then to use each as a base for village exploration. (From a strict geographical standpoint, the coast itself divides into three sections —the estuarial dunes backed by alluvial tracts; the Morte Bay coast, including the two great horns that mark its northern and southern extremities; the hog-backed cliffs that front the Severn Sea—but the character of the villages is better seen in a different perspective.)

The Barnstaple-Ilfracombe road boxes in the western coast. The northern coast runs from Ilfracombe to County Gate, where Devon ends. The hilly centre of North Devon might—as local patriotism dictates—be placed at either Shirwell, Muddiford or Bittadon. East, most of the villages in the skirts of Exmoor cling to the sides of combes down which flow rapid streams born on the moorland top. If the area is explored by a traveller who systematically works his way through those four 'sub-districts' a degree of uniformity can be perceived within the diversity. The character of each distinct zone emerges.

Immediately west of Barnstaple the road to Braunton draws its long, slow length along the shore of the estuary threading through alluvial land where the pastures are rich and where, in the northern extremity, Braunton Great Field still displays surviving features of the open field and strip cultivation system that the Saxons established. Here, specialist flower crops and glasshouse tomatoes are the main products. Braunton itself is too large to be included in this book, but on its way to that place the road skirts pleasant little Ashford standing high on its hill and gazing delightedly out over the widening waters, a big camping and caravan site between it and the lazy river. Further down and on the other side of the road the famous R.A.F. base at Chivenor makes a very special kind of village and, in the civilian settlement, a busy woodworking industry has been established within the last ten years.

Heanton Punchardon ('the high farm held by Robert de Ponte Cardonis—"Robert Thistle Bridge" ') is a textbook example of a lie-of-the-land village, shaped quite clearly to follow the contours of the ridge on which it stands. It has a lovely church, light, bright and graceful, full of fascinating monuments. In the graveyard the 'Postman-Poet's' tomb attracts a lot of attention. The bell that he used to ring to announce his arrival when out on his huge rural round is set in the stone. Edward Capern was born at Tiverton in 1819 and started work in the lace factory there when he was 8. Bad eyesight forced him to leave that employment and he endured poverty until he found work as a rural letter carrier, based on Bideford. Not that his hard times were then over, for he had a wife and family to support on a wage of 10s. 6d. a week. He composed his verses while out on his round, and in 1856 the warm-hearted Frederick William Rock of Barnstaple organized their publication. Capern's sentimental ditties suited the public taste and sold well. (The post office was so moved that it raised his wages to 13s. a week and excused him Sunday duty.) One of these early poems called "The Lion Flag of England" was circulated as a broadsheet to sustain the morale of the troops in the Crimea, and Capern was awarded a Civil List pension of £40 a year. After this, he never looked back. Book followed book. He is quite forgotten now and his poetry is as silent as his bell.

At Braunton the B3231 heads west for the sea, skirting the northern end of Saunton's famous sands. Here, in fact, is one of the few parts of the coast to justify the name 'Golden Coast' which, in the jargon of the day, is being *promoted* by the North Devon Tourist Association. Naturally, its attractions to the holiday-makers and tourists are seen as outweighing its manifest geographical inaccuracies when applied to a coast which, throughout its entire length, is chiefly remarkable for a superb cliff wall, very rarely breached. The enunciation of this simple truth in no way detracts from the splendour of the two extensive beaches at Saunton and at Woolacombe. Nor does it indicate any failure to appreciate the delights of a coast the majesty of which cannot be surpassed; and will certainly not be lessened by catchpenny slogans.

Beyond the sands, the road loops round the first of the headlands and curves inland to Croyde. The best authorities agree that the village took its name from the stream on which it stands, but earlier writers told a romantic story of two Norse raiders who made a landing on the shores of the bay. One—Crida—gave his name to Croyde: the other—Putta—left his memory preserved in the nearby Putsborough. Croyde has other problems on its hands just now. It desperately fears the expansion of the Ruda

Caravan Park, dreading that the personality of the delightful village will be overwhelmed. Croyde Parish Council argues that further development here will be an encroachment on the county council's own coastal preservation plans, but so far neither the county council nor the Minister of the Environment will give Croyde the support to which it feels entitled. The problem is typical of Devon's dilemma. The superb natural amenities of the county attract visitors. Visitors have become a vital element in its economy. The more visitors, the greater the threat to peace and beauty. Nobody who has seen the hideous deterioration of Devon's south coast over the past twenty years can fail to sympathize with Croyde.

It may be that the battle has come too late. Many would argue that Croyde is already a resort rather than a village—there is a world of difference between the two—its old, lovely core buried beneath layers of touristic development. Croyde's fine surfing beach has certainly proved a magnet; but inland, the village itself retains 'atmosphere'. The little stream runs through an attractive cottage street, so close to the houses that they have little 'bridges' at their front doors. There are two good pubs and one of these— the Manor Inn—gave rise to the tradition of the 'Mayors of Croyde'. It was not unusual for a departing customer to fall into the stream, becoming by that involuntary act 'Mayor of Croyde' and retaining the title until another gay-goer suffered the same misadventure and thereby relieved him of his unsought office.

Georgeham, in whose parish Croyde lies, is much less vulnerable than Croyde, being further inland. The 'sea mania' of the twentieth century has brought about a return—though bloodless—of the dangers of the Dark Ages. The seaboard is vulnerable again: from holiday-makers now, not from sea-borne raiders. Georgeham has seen its church twice and violently 'restored' in its long history. In 1762 it was 'classized' and in 1876 it was 're-gothicized'. There are some intriguing monuments inside the church. The registers are in outstanding condition; and, in the graveyard, most delightful to behold, the tombs of Sergeant John Hill, of the 40th Regiment of Infantry—'a Waterloo man'—and, very pathetically, of Philip Goss whose doggerel little verse is a sad commentary on human life. It is of interest that the old habit of rhyming epitaphs has been continued into modern times in Georgeham.

Not far away, Putsborough would not be lightly challenged if it claimed to be the possessor of the loveliest manor house in all England. Surrounded by trees, and standing in a beautiful garden, the house is ringed with its own clear water which finally tumbles through an opening in the garden wall and makes a 'splash' across the narrow road. Putsborough Manor House and the twelfth-century chapel at Croyde are ample reward for a leisurely ramble through this quiet countryside.

Baggy Point, the southern horn of Morte Bay, is sublime and will remain so—seal and seabird haunted—as long as man, the great destroyer, will allow it to be. The promontory was raised from the ocean bed in what, to the geologist, are recent times. Its rocks are an intrusion between the Pickwell Down sandstones to the north and the Pilton Beds to the south. It was as a result of the elevation of Baggy Point that the old cliff line further north—now represented by the bluffs of Woolacombe Down—retreated inland out of the water and so facilitated the creation of Woola-combe Sands. The waves were no longer able to attack these cliffs, and the old boulders were ground down into fine sand.

Well, this may be the 'Golden Coast'—and Woolacombe is without doubt one of the finest beaches in England—but it is a dangerous coast. Cliff-walled or sand-footed, it is perilous, and holiday-makers would be well-advised to heed the warning notices. On 1st August 1971, for example, nine swimmers and paddlers—would have been swept out to sea from these 'Golden Sands' if the lifeguards had not been alert, courageous and skilful.

In the summer when, from far over Brendon Top and all the way along from Blackmoor Gate, the roads are crawling with cars and caravans, it seems incongruous to recall the antiquity of Woolacombe and Mortehoe. And even there, on the ground, it is almost impossible to recapture the romance of these places. But from autumn through to spring imagination is not needed. The sea, the rocks and the gales reclaim their own when the visitors have gone.

Round Morte Point, where jagged teeth threatened embayed vessels, the north coast proper—hog-backed and lonely—begins: a lighthouse at Bull Point and nothing but cove-clinging hamlets and quiet bartons from here to Ilfracombe.

East of that popular resort lies the charming village of Berrynarbor, reached by a steep road running up the lower reaches of the Sterridge Valley where a trout stream cascades over little weirs and sparkles under the crowding hazels. The settlement nestles very snugly beneath a hill. St Peter's—a fine church, with outstanding furniture and memorials—is raised well above the level of the thatched cottages. Not for away, at Bowden Farm, a very remarkable man was born. Bishop Jewel fled from England in the reign of Mary and returned when Elizabeth was on the throne. His *Apology for the Church of England* (1562) was one of the great theological disputations of that (or indeed of any) age.

Combe Martin—strawberry-growing, silver-bearing Combe Martin, the next settlement east—is too big to be included here. It is a resort now, at least for three months of the year. The only true coastal villages left (for lovely Lynmouth must be taken with ancient Lynton) are Trentishoe and Martinhoe—and the two combined would hardly add up to more than a hamlet, were it not that anything larger than a single house or churchtown counts as a village on this wonderfully lonely coast. They are sublimely sited, sharing in the unique quality of this magnificent stretch of countryside, where cliffs hang over the sea and the moorland comes down to the cliffs. They flank the splendid valley, or cleave, as it is better called, running to the sea at Heddon's mouth; and north of Martinhoe are the remains of a Roman signal station where a small garrison kept watch for intruding and recalcitrant Silures who, unlike the Dumnonii, had not accepted the Pax Romana. Though post-war ploughing has destroyed some of the moorland here, the district and its little settlements retain great beauty and interest.

Lynton and Lynmouth are both old and new, for both were 'discovered' and 'developed' comparatively late, a fact that gives Lynton a predominantly Victorian and Edwardian appearance and dilutes Lynmouth's rural air with a good deal of later hotel building. Lynton, having acquired urban status, cannot fitly occupy space here, but the two places are so intimately linked by geography and history that one cannot be mentioned without the other.

Lynton's nineteenth-century architecture reflects the virtual isolation of this part of North Devon's coast before road and railway building enabled the holiday-makers to arrive. Agriculture and fishing provided a scanty living for a small population, and the little vessels that tied up at Lynmouth brought in most of what the outside world needed to supply. For the rest, pannier ponies struggled over the moorland tracks and maintained tenuous links with Barnstaple and Porlock. Early man, in fact, left more permanent memorials than did his medieval successors. Both the cliff tops, the stupendous valleys and the bare moorland heights bear a wealth of barrows, standing-stones and 'castles'.

Until the tourist traffic began, the grazing of the moorland commons, the raising of store cattle and the growing of oats and rye for home consumption were the chief occupations of Lynton folk, and to these activities Lynmouth added its own speciality of herring fishing and curing. Fortunately, as the herring shoals departed the human shoals arrived.

It is not possible to exaggerate the picturesqueness of Lynmouth. The narrow valley, a rapid river and tree-filled slopes: the little harbour, the Rhenish Tower, the majesty of the Foreland (now, happily, National Trust property), the fascinating cliff railway, the thatch and cob, the dizzily-perched hotels, the splendid 'Rising Sun'. Naturally, it gets crowded in the summer. I am lucky and can see it in spring or autumn.

The terrible flood of 1952—born on Exmoor's brooding Chains —is a receding memory. Not only Lynmouth but inland Barbrook and many another of Exmoor's villages were devastated. Thirty-one people lost their lives and ninety-three houses were destroyed. The scars have healed, the flood-prevention engineering has proved effective, time has assuaged grief. Even so, the Orchard Theatre's proposal to commemorate the event in drama, twenty years later, encountered sharp hostility from the Lynton Council. "Let us forget," they said. It is the river itself that provides a perpetual reminder. Here at Lynmouth every river that flows north off Exmoor reaches the sea, for here the East and West Lyn, to which they are all tributary, join and flow in one course through the village and into the harbour. Heavy rain on the moor—and the Chains average ninety inches—turns the clear water chocolate brown, roaring (harmlessly now) down its boulder-strewn bed and fanning out misfeaturedly into the clearer waters of the Severn Sea.

The deep and wooded valley of the Yeo forms the eastern boundary of that central upland portion of North Devon, where, though not far away, neither coast nor moorland wields dominion.

M

From the Yeo west to the A361 is a land of marked and individual character. Rolling, rising high in the north, and nowhere low-lying, the soil has responded well to modern farming and though the holdings are usually small to medium there is much evidence of improving pasture and established plough. A good way of dis-covering for oneself this 'mid-north-Devon feel' is to journey from Ashford, close to and overlooking the Taw and typical of these estuary villages, to Marwood only two miles away. Only two miles, but in a different world—a world of wooded combes, rounded downs and Saxon farmhouses. Despite the agricultural advances already mentioned, the area gives an impression of stability and timeless self-possession. Change there has been, but change of rate not of direction. The life-patterns traced out here were established centuries ago. Among many fine examples, Westcott Barton stands out as a superb Domesday manor. Complete with its own mill, the farmhouse and buildings bear unmistakable evidence of medieval work which the rebuilding of 1600 made no attempt to obliterate. Marwood's splendid church tells in its various styles and century-spanning monuments the story of this rural com-munity. What I like best here is an example of the work of John Berry, a famous sundial maker. On the south porch was mounted in 1762 one of his masterpieces. It shows the time in the principal cities of Europe—in Jerusalem—*and* in Marwood!

West Down, a big and splendidly-planned village on the western fringes of the area, is neighboured (if the word can be used appropriately in a sparsely settled land) by Bittadon, tucked neatly away in a lovely valley. The hills around team with Bronze Age barrows to which time, and man, have been kinder than they have to St Peter's, whose squat, dunce's-capped tower prepares the visitor for the badly 'restored' interior.

Shirwell is old enough and was once important enough to give its name to a hundred. Well, it's quiet now. A good church, in which Chichester monuments remind us of the longevity of both 'known' and 'unknown' families in these parts. Chichesters were at Youlston from Tudor times to the early twentieth century. Another branch was at Westcott from the seventeenth century. Poyntzes and Aclands were at Bittadon, while at Arlington (further up the Yeo from Shirwell) the main branch of the Chichesters lived from the fourteenth century (they acquired it by marriage to a Raleigh) until the estate was handed over to the National Trust in 1947. The house itself isn't much (1820-ish) but the grounds are magnificent and the coach and cart museum is a delight.

East of the Yeo the moorland feel deepens at every mile. For example, the National Park boundary is three miles away from Bratton Fleming but, for me at any rate, it is most certainly in the skirts of the moorland, though far less obviously 'an Exmoor village' than either Parracombe or Challacombe. It is a biggish, straggling, one-street village with a church about which the experts find little to praise except for its plate; and the village itself has no great architectural features. It is, however, the home of a scholar to whose studies and writings hundreds of enquirers are indebted. Charles Whybrow knows more about this northern part of Devon than any other student and is generous in help to all who ask. His work on the parish of Bratton has uncovered a wealth of detail illuminating the past and enriching the present— and this has been but a fraction of his scholarly labour.

At Chelfham, the old and now dismantled Barnstaple-Lynton railway used to cross the Stoke Rivers valley at its junction with the Yeo on a stupendous viaduct, four hundred feet long and seventy feet in the air. What a vast undertaking for a line that, in its best years, paid shareholders a half per cent dividend! In the twenties the motor car began to take away what little traffic the L & B.R. had. In 1935 it closed down at the end of the summer season. It was one of the most picturesque railways in Britain, and—especially in Bratton parish—faced great working problems. Parts of the old and lovely route can still be walked but, as in the case of most of our abandoned lines, the opportunity to create uninterrupted 'through-ways' for walkers, cyclists and riders has been lost.

Between Bratton Fleming and the Wistlandpound reservoir a long, uncertain road leads past farms whose names are celebrated in Exmoor's most famous hunting song and are often said to be 'typical Devonshire': Southacott, Knightacott, Sprecott, Hunnacott. While not denying their attractiveness, especially in the song—"Knightacott, Narracott, Hunnacott past . . ."—it is necessary to point out that they are certainly not typical of Devon

as a whole. These *cott* (and *worthy*) names occur chiefly in the
northern zone, round the moorland edges. The Saxon colonists
ringed the moor round with their settlements, establishing very
few 'up top'—Pinkworthy is an exception—and the *cott* and
worthy terminations indicate that these early farmers came from
Somerset.

Eastwards and higher, stands Challacombe, just inside the
National Park boundary and only a mile and a half from the
Edgerley Stone, where Somerset begins. Some say the name means
'cold valley', others that it means 'calves' valley'. Either interpretation has much to recommend it, for the wind is never still here
and the moorland raises good beef cattle. For certain, the Celts
lived here, long after the Saxons came. *Combe* is a British word
and in the parish there's a farm called Wallover Barton—'the farm
of the Wealas'. The Challacombe that everybody knows is on the
roadside; a cluster of cottages, post office, a farm or two and the
excellent 'Black Venus'. Until 1967 the pub was called the 'Ring
of Bells' but was then renamed by its present owner and landlord. He says that it was known as the 'Black Venus' in 1812,
then as the 'New Inn'. When the church bells were rehung in
1845 the name was changed again to celebrate that event, pubs
and churches customarily working together in village life. However, Charles Whybrow, working on information supplied by Jack
Huxtable of Swincombe—whose family has farmed here for many
generations—is convinced that the name 'Black Venus' never
applied to the inn. One of Jack Huxtable's ancestors married
Joseph Webber—Webbers still live in Challacombe—and the
family papers show that Edward Webber (1746–1847: yes, he
really did live as long as that) made testamentary disposition of
a property called 'Black Venus', which has been identified as one
of two houses about two hundred yards south of the inn. There
was also a small meadow called by the same name.

It is an interesting story. Nobody, of course, disputes the owner's
right to call his property what he likes; and, incidentally, nobody
who visits the inn will ever regret doing so. The mystery remains,
however, of how so exotic a name ever came to be attached to
either a house or a meadow in this little Exmoor village. Being
deeply conservative in such matters, I was, at first, dismayed when
the inn's name was changed. Now, I'm rather in favour of it. It

perpetuates—and in delightful fashion—a very remarkable Exmoor name that few people could ever have heard of.

The principal part of Challacombe—the 'church town'—is away from the main road. First, there's a straggle of houses, then the road makes a big bend round the hilltop, and there is the church and the mill and deep peace.

Parracombe ('valley marked by an enclosure'?) is Challacombe's northern neighbour and much the most interesting way of getting from one to the other is on foot over the moorland tracks. (I don't suppose that anybody will take my advice.) Then you come into Parracombe past the Chapman Barrows, probably Exmoor's finest cluster, and enter by Church Town and St Petrock's. This is the old church—eleventh-century—abandoned in 1878 when it was feared to be unsafe and a new church was built in the main part of the village. Its most remarkable feature is neither its age nor its decay, but its completely unspoilt interior. Its abandonment in 1878 prevented the Victorians from ruining it. Eighteenth-century box-pews (a few sixteenth-century as well), an eighteenth-century screen, a Georgian pulpit and, at the west end, the old church musicians' gallery—very Hardyesque. Wooden hatpegs on the walls and oval tablets bearing urbane hortations, a simple, whitewashed interior where no lines are straight; a complete and wonderfully interesting building.

In 1968 St Petrock's had to be closed to visitors because it was near collapse. The Redundant Churches Fund, most commendably concerned for the welfare of such a gem, put extensive repairs in hand and it is now safe again and properly restored. (It is, however, too often locked still, I notice.) It is unlikely to be re-dedicated but the ancient Revels services will be held there again. The famous Whitsun Revels of Parracombe always took place on Church Town green right by the church, near what must have been one of the loveliest church houses in Devon.

Parracombe's other treasure is Holwell Castle; a textbook example, says Charles Whybrow, of a motte and bailey. It's a surprising sight in this peaceful place. But Parracombe repays close exploration and I'd suggest basing oneself at the 'Fox and Goose'.

The road out of Parracombe swoops north, then east. Big curves were forced on the engineers, for the north Exmoor combes are precipitous and, in any case, this road is traversing hog-backed cliffs in a land where rivers fall fifteen hundred feet in less than four miles. There is no road in Britain that offers lovelier views than the coast road of Exmoor.

At Barbrook there is a choice of routes, north to Lynton or east (with many a hairpin on the way) to Hillsford Bridge and Waters Meet or, later, south then east again into the lovely Brendon valley. Here, before long, as visitors increase as they infallibly will, some sort of 'travel rationing' will become essential in the summer. Perhaps a Goyt valley scheme or a one-way system. These beautiful water-bordered lanes cannot much longer endure the seasonal pressure to which they are subjected.

The whole area is a honeypot—'Doone Country'. Rockford straggles along a narrow lane: some pleasant cottages, a nice pub, gift shops, woods, water, the deer (when the visitors have gone!). Brendon church is far enough out of the village—wonderful views from the churchyard—to make attendance a real test of devotion. Brendon itself ('bramble hill'?—or, possibly from St Brendan the sixth-century Irish saint to whom the church is dedicated) is remarkable less for its buildings than for its situation and its legends. For this little place was the centre of Doone stories long before Blackmore wrote his novel. Every visitor longs to see 'the Doone Valley' (and has the haziest notion of where it is) and the church 'where Lorna was married and shot' (that is at Oare, in the 'wrong' county). But at least Lorna Doone Farm at Malmsmead can be found. A lovely building in an idyllic setting (Badgworthy Water flows under its bridge), it has the unusual distinction of catering for the needs of thousands of tourists without sacrifice of beauty, dignity or quality. This is a rare achievement. Those who wish to can set off from here for moorland walks or rides up an incomparable valley. At the farm itself, they will find good food and wine, a museum of great interest and a shop of rare quality. The vulgarization that—in tourist areas—is so often the price paid for success is completely missing here.

The southern ridge of Exmoor is a long rampart running out of Devon and into Somerset, for the latter takes a great bite out of its neighbour in Exmoor country. In the narrowing strip between the county boundary and the A361 a handful of villages sit in the southern skirts of Devon Exmoor.

In the deeply-wooded Bray valley, Brayford, High Bray and Charles illustrate between them many of the geographical diversities and the historic developments of what is superficially an empty and quiet land. Big quarries remind us of the many mining ventures here—both failures and successes—in a countryside where most of the minerals useful to man are found. High Bray—it's a topographical name—has a church that the Normans established and the Victorians finished. And all around are the barrows and the Domesday farms. Charles was the rocky place where a Celtic princeling had his rude palace and survived the Saxon storm. Blackmore stayed here as a boy, for his grandfather and uncle were persons at High Bray and Charles respectively. The old man was the patron, as well as, at one time, the incumbent of Charles, but chose not to bestow the living on Blackmore's father, selecting the younger brother for preferment.

A few miles east at Heasley Mill a vast mining enterprise flourished in the late nineteenth century. The Florence, Bampfylde, Britannia and Crowbarn mines produced huge quantities of iron and copper between 1870 and 1890. By 1900 they were all 'knocked'. Only the spoil heaps and adits remain to remind the visitor of the days when two hundred miners, mostly Irish, Welsh and Cornish, laboured there, arriving at South Molton every Saturday night to spend their wages and to beat the place up.

North Molton was also connected with the Heasley mines; in fact, tradition claims that Germans were brought over in Elizabeth I's reign to work the rich deposits. There is to this day something of a mining village atmosphere in North Molton, though its main source of wealth, apart from agriculture, was its Tudor woollen industry, killed by the Napoleonic Wars. Once a royal manor, centre of a hundred and a (non-incorporated) borough, the little place wears a sort of Dogberry-ish air: ". . . a fellow that hath had losses . . . and [yet] everything handsome about him". The little square, the houses, the 'Poltimore Arms', the school and church make a pleasing composition (but for the wretched tangle of overhead wires). All Saints has a mighty tower and its interior is worthy of that lovely structure. The pulpit, 'wineglass' with Hanoverian sounding board, is said to be one of the finest in Devon. Richard Bampfylde's tomb bears a striking tribute to his and his wife's fecundity: twelve sons and five daughters. The old church clock's works are preserved and well deserve to be. The timepiece was made in Barnstaple in 1564 at the cost of £6 13s. 4d. It was in good going order until 1934.

Court Barton, just west of the church, is a fine sixteenth-century house. Lytton Strachey stayed there with a reading party in March 1909. He wrote with enthusiasm about "its mild tranquilities" which seem to have consisted of "a surplusage of beef and Devonshire cream . . . a village shop with bulls'-eyes . . . more cream, and then more beef, and then somnolence. . . ." He expressed some bewilderment at not being able to see the moorland. Strangers to Exmoor never realize how secretive the moor can be. These little villages tucked away in the foothills seem a thousand miles away from 'the Forest', yet their lives are bound up with it.

Twitchen ('the meeting of the two ways') and Molland ('bare, round-topped hill') are each representative, in different ways, of these isolated places. Twitchen is far too small to be a village but deserves mention as showing how vital the old tracks were. It exists—and has a church—simply because the two ways met there. In country such as this—and wheeled vehicles were unknown on Exmoor as late as the seventeenth century—the junction of two pannier-pony and packmen routes was bound to attract settlement. Molland is much bigger, and its Celtic name demonstrates its antiquity. If only for two things it must always be dear to the lover of Exmoor: the London Inn—oh, surprising name!— and St Mary's church, as utterly unspoilt as Parracombe's St Petrock's. Here you will find box-pews, whitewashed walls, three-decker pulpit, hat-pegs, Georgian screen, and royal arms that blazon the names of their painter, Rowlands, and the church-warden, Mogridge, who, in 1808, saw no reason why they should not share in the glory. Parson Froude preached here and they can still tell you stories of his legendary deeds.

East of Molland and as far east as the twisting, baffling county boundary there are no more true villages in this part of Devon. Hamlets like the Ansteys and Morebath; single farms; tiny cottage clusters—these in plenty. But this most quiet and most empty part of Devon ends in a tract where people are few and silence broods.

It is not unfitting that this rapid and imperfect survey of Devon villages should end in such a country and on such a note, for the fate of the village itself is in the balance. A few, with the demise of the railways and the failure of rural bus services, are regaining the marketing and servicing importance that they had down to the late eighteenth century; but they are the exceptions. Many, particularly the coastal villages, are given over to tourism and the provision of week-end accommodation—but this is not village life as we have known it.

For most, the future must be problematical. The re-establishment of cottage industries—the ideal solution—seems unlikely and agriculture can never again be a labour-intensive industry. The 'estate village' is an anachronism today; fishing is concentrated where landing, refrigerating, packaging, marketing and distributing facilities are available. Mining is unlikely to return to many now-silent places that were once dependent upon mineral wealth.

It is on such a questioning note that we must end. Has the village a function in our modern world? Not, I think, while we pursue our present materialistic aims and worship the twin gods of mass-production and mass-consumption. The restoration of the village to its old importance depends upon a social and economic revolution which in its turn—some would say—demands so profound a questioning of our values as to be quite beyond the realm of possibility. Certain it is that in a society more—and necessarily more—'planned' the revival of the village plays no part in our forward thinking.

The type of community that for well over a thousand years was unquestioningly accepted as man's 'natural' home has been—I think for ever—displaced from its central position; and that even in the most rural of counties—Defenascir!

Index